129

Signed - 2000

To Betty

who says the nicest
things to me!
Thanks

Stan Delaplane

THE LITTLE WORLD
OF STANTON DELAPLANE

Also by Stanton Delaplane   **POSTCARDS FROM DELAPLANE**

THE

LITTLE WORLD
OF
STANTON DELAPLANE

Being Stanton Delaplane's

observations of

the lighter side of life

on our small planet. . .

Coward-McCann, Inc.

New York

© 1959 BY STANTON DELAPLANE

Decorations by David McKay

Library of Congress Catalog
Card Number: 59-6093

These columns originally appeared in the *San Francisco Chronicle* and various newspapers serviced by the McNaught Syndicate.

MANUFACTURED IN THE UNITED STATES OF AMERICA

This book is for
KRISTIN—
Who always wondered
What in the world
Her father did
For a living.

CONTENTS

THE OLD WORLD

THE NEW WORLD

OUT BEYOND THE WEST

THE OLD WORLD

FRANCE

There is nothing like Paris in the Spring. The trees along the boulevards all trembling in the fresh spring breeze. The cleaning crews washing down the sidewalks in the cool Paris dawn. The sidewalk cafés at sunset with the crowded tables under the gay awnings. And the Paris nights, flamed with neon and bright with music spilling out of the gay cafés.

The great gray stone buildings along the Seine. The late afternoon smash of cars and little square red taxis along the Rue Royal and the Champs Elysées. The trim Paris police in stiff caps and blue uniforms twirling the traffic along with white batons and amazingly even tempers.

The parade of sleek ladies with clipped poodles. The breathtaking swirl of traffic around the Place de la Concorde. The gleam of silver and white cloth in the great restaurants. And the flavor of Normandy sole and fresh water cress. The wines of Vouvray and fresh strawberry tart and French coffee. And the fragrant apple brandy of Calvados.

"The merry merry month of May"

Sunday is the best day to go to the Place du Tertre. The sunny little square lies in a cobblestone street. Surrounded by wine shops, artists and tourists.

The buildings sag on ancient foundations. The whole scene looks like a stage set.

When I arrived, a goat was climbing a red ladder with a monkey on his back.

My young lady of ten years was bug-eyed. This is the Paris she came to see.

The Place du Tertre is surrounded by artistic taverns. Such as Le Grenier, the Cadet Gascogne and Patachou where the patrons join in the chorus of off-color salle-de-garde songs.

On Sunday, restaurants like La Mère Catherine and Chez Eugene set up tables in the square under the trees. Somebody ran a long wire through the street and up into an apartment. And when they turned on the record player, so help me it was Leadbelly.

Half a dozen artists had set up easels in the streets. They wore turtle-neck sweaters and were artistically dirty. They stabbed at the canvas with palette knives and with fingers. It is not artistic to use a brush.

In the center of the square, a gentleman performed rapid

cuts on paper with scissors. When he unfolded it, it became a complicated lacy pattern tablecloth.

Everybody drank wine and clapped. The monkey got off the goat's back. The goat climbed down the ladder and went into La Mère Catherine's. Possibly for a short one before lunch.

The goat-and-monkey man and the tablecloth man passed among the crowd, holding out their hats for money.

The sun came down warm. And the waitress from Chez Eugene's brought us a little turquoise pottery pitcher full of chilled Alsatian wine.

Across the street there was a shop hung with brilliant colored etchings. You could pick up a fine print for about 60 cents.

The ten-year-old disappeared into this art center for postcards. And when I went over to get her, I found her absorbed in a corner over a stack of nude ladies in artistic poses.

"They have no clothes on," she said.

"Why, so they haven't," I said. "But then possibly they live in a hot climate."

"Lucky," she said enviously. She likes to go around bare as a radish in summer.

"Why do they sell these postcards?" she said.

Well, I believe in frank answers for the young.

"Why," I said, "they are purchased by tourist gentlemen who then inscribe them 'Having a wonderful time. Wish you were here.' It is very humorous."

"I don't think it is so funny," she said.

"Neither do I," I said firmly. "Would you give me half a dozen, ma'am. In a plain wrapper," I told the lady at the counter.

The lady at Chez Eugene's brought us roast chicken with a light flavor of estragon. The salad of cucumbers must have grown up in the dressing.

The goat and monkey came out of La Mère Catherine's a little unsteadily. They went up the ladder again.

"Tomorrow," I told the young lady, "we will go to the Louvre. And to other classy museums where your father is well known as a patron."

"I don't want to," she said. "I want to come right back here. Who are you going to send the postcards to?"

"Oh, Mr. Rex Smith, the airlines gentleman you met in New York. And Mr. Walter Ramage, the hotel gentleman in Reno. And many others of our friends.

"Because," I said cheerfully, "we are having a wonderful time. And we do wish they were here, don't we?"

Calf and calvados

The Paris papers I find are filled with very daffy material. About daffy people. Such as cryptic statements from Mr. Aly Khan about why he will not speak about the Riviera. And how Farouk flings ladies' slippers so that they catch on the shelf behind the bar. And wins and loses many francs.

And how all the fancy Dans from the States hang about such people. And truly it is enough to turn the milk in my café complet these mornings.

Well, that is beside the point. The point is I was lunching at Fouquet the other day. Fouquet is a most posh outdoor café at the corner of Champs Elysées and George V. And thus it is much frequented by such people.

I was lunching with Mr. Benn Reyes of Chicago and Mr. Arthur Schurgin of Detroit. And with Mr. Jim Nolan, the agent de presse for Europe. And gandering the menu whereon my eye revealed "tête de veau." Calf head, that is.

There are door handles that hit you in the head when you bend over.

The faucet in the tub has a thermometer on it so you can set the temperature of incoming water. How classy can you get?

Well, ask a question and you get an answer. The Duke and Duchess of Windsor have come to Paris from New York.

They have leased a 30-room house in the Bois de Boulogne.

If this gets crowded, they can move out to a converted mill in the valley of the Chevreuse at Gif-sur-Yvette.

The Duchess's bathrooms have been decorated by Dimitri Bouchene, a Russian stage designer. French bathrooms are pretty big. I guess you could put on a one-set play in them if you wanted to.

In the town house bathroom, he put in murals of mauve, pale blue and deep crimson. A lot of figures are racing around the walls, half human, half animal.

For the bathroom in the country, Dimitri hung a clothesline. He did not hang it with socks and shirts like my bathroom. He hung it with Japanese lanterns, balloons, gloves and scarves.

This sounds impractical to me. About the last thing I need when shaving is a Japanese lantern on a clothesline. I want light. If I can find the switch.

In French restaurants and night clubs, the powder room is coeducational. This is remarkably cozy if you get used to it. I never have.

The powder room is run by a lady. She follows you around in the most solicitous way you can imagine.

While you are wishing your hands, she sneaks up behind you and sprays your hair with Fleur de Robert Mitchum. Couple of ladies from the table next to you come in and chat.

The first time I walked into this situation, I thought the

The French gentleman at the table could not explain it exactly in English. But he said it was delicious.

"Probably something like head cheese," said Mr. Reyes.

"I will take it," I said.

Now I assume that a good many people know how wrong I was. But for people like me, I will explain.

For tête de veau, they take one calf head. They boil it and serve it with a dressing of oil and vinegar.

It is extremely lifelike and distressing. My tête de veau came in with one ear cocked. As if he were listening for the telephone to ring.

"It is delicious," said the Frenchman diving into his.

My friends were most unsympathetic. They urged me to eat up every cheek and jowl. Lest I offend the French gentleman and undo all the international diplomacy of Mr. Dulles.

"Why don't you try singing to it?" said Mr. Reyes, pointing to the ear.

The tête de veau had something of the consistency of a boiled bedroom slipper. It was well greased with oil and had a tendency to skate over the tongue.

I tried not to look at the ear and got down a mouthful or two.

"Delicious," I murmured.

"Why don't you get the waiter to put a scoop of ice cream in the ear?" Mr. Schurgin suggested.

"Or he could put in a few roses like a vase," said Mr. Reyes. Both of them had ordered roast beef.

"I am afraid you do not like it," said the French gentleman.

"On the contrary," I said.

"Why don't you have them start cooking another?" said Mr. Reyes helpfully.

And so with one thing and another, we got down to the ear. Which I left on my plate, pleading nolo contendere and no appetite. And told the waiter to hustle me up some coffee and calvados, the Normandy apple brandy that cuts any taste.

And the only reason I mention this is to point out that I hang around with a fast international set at Fouquet.

But I do not fling ladies' slippers with King Farouk. Or mouse about getting nonsense statements from Mr. Aly Khan. Or behave in other silly ways that the international set behaves in.

No, sir, I sit about and eat the tête de veau. And promote international good will and hands across the sea. Even though it makes me seasick.

Number, please

Paris is a wonderful town and priced about equal to New York. Who can afford New York, unless you live there?

The chestnut trees are budding out. Just as though they were under contracts to Tin Pan Alley. The optimistic French are sitting at the sidewalk cafés. Still bundled in topcoats, but hopeful.

The Parisian dogs trot snootily along the boulevards. And the sidewalk kiosks are a glitter of varnished cover magazines.

The French telephones, I must report, are as widely unpredictable as ever.

"N'hesitez pas à telephoner au concierge si au cours de la nuit vous êtes réveillé par des bruits anormaux."

That is what it says on my telephone. Under the plastic.

I translate this to mean: "Don't hesitate to pipe the concierge if in the course of the night you are awakened by enormous brutes."

At the Scribe Hotel on Rue Scribe at Boulevard des Cap cines, the pay telephones are as mysterious as atomic energ

First you "mettez le jeton." It took me some time to fi out that a "jeton" is a thin slug. I tried one-franc pieces, fi franc pieces made of pot metal. Twenty-franc pieces. I tri sideways and upside down. I was trying to stuff in a dollar b when the washroom lady came out and gave me a slug.

After you "mettez le jeton," you lift the receiver. And fro there on it is a simple dial matter. Until your party answe Your party cannot hear you until you push a button whic mettezes the jeton down into the pay box.

Consequently you hear them crying, "Allo, Allo, Allo While you cry "Allo" into a dead box. This way you lo plenty jetons without much action.

The "Uncle, Sugar, Able" spelling we learned at Gover ment expense during the war gets slightly perfumed whe handled in French.

Gentleman who spelled my name for reservations by phor the other day unloaded as follows: "Duhlahplahn. D f Denise, E for Étienne, L for Louise, A for André, P for Pierre And so on.

Makes you feel like you're covered with hair tonic.

Cold hands, hot water

I am a veteran of the French bathroom. The French bat tub is built like a swimming pool. It is half a mile down th hall.

The bathroom lights are in unpredictable places. For a lon time I shaved in half-darkness. Until one day I dropped th razor and discovered a switch under the bowl. It turned o enough light to play night baseball.

waiter had framed me. I was all for going out and tossing him up for grabs.

But the lady in charge seized me.

"Ici, monsieur," she said smiling.

"Why, ma'am," I said. "I was just passing by and thought I'd say howdy. I am shy as Hopalong Cassidy," I said, "and if you will pardon me, ma'am, I will just hop along."

The lady hung a towel over my arm. She pushed me inside. She sprayed me with liquid flowers.

"Voilà!" she said.

"You ain't just a-whistlin' Dixie," I murmured.

You are supposed to drop 100 francs on the plate as you leave. Fifty will do in less plush places.

Well, I have played the Japanese deep-dish bath. And I have done a pretty complete job out of a helmet and done my laundry in it afterward. I am not easily surprised.

I have never quite got used to straightening my tie alongside ladies who are putting on make-up. That is all.

I remember well stepping into a dual control powder room in the Rue Duphot. Lady standing at the mirror finished the make-up job.

I bent over to adjust my shoelace to cover my confusion. But the lady paid me no attention. Just adjusted something in the hopalong holster area that snapped into place with a loud pop. She walked out as though I weren't there with my mouth open.

Trouble is they don't put signs on these places. Like they do in the States. Like *His* and *Hers*. I guess if they did, they would just mark it *Theirs*.

The bon voyage

The other day I stepped up to the window at Thos. Cook & Son, agence de voyages, to exchange a few dollars for francs.

"I have a letter of credit," I began.

"Pardon, monsieur?"

"A letter of credit—"

"Of course, monsieur. Through the little door over there." After a while I came back.

"I want the letter of credit department," I said desperately.

"But monsieur," he said, "that is the toilette. Through the little door."

"You don't seem to get the idea," I said. "It is a matter of money."

"Ah, monsieur," he said proudly. "For this service, Thos. Cook & Son charges absolutely nothing."

That is the problem of traveling. Nobody understands you. Speak English and you find yourself among the washbasins. Speak French and they think you are speaking broken English.

French taxis do not have ash trays. I found one though the other day while riding the front seat. As I flipped the ash, the driver let out a great cry of despair.

"Mais, non, monsieur," he said. "That is where I keep my change."

"Jolie madame"

Nearly everybody in Paris is showing fashions or going to see them. The other day I went over to Balmain at François Ier, 44, to see what's haute with the haute couture.

"I wish you had asked me for tickets earlier," said Mr. Art Buchwald, the Paris columnist. "You have to apply two weeks in advance for the press showing. The press showing is the most fun."

"Why?" I said.

"Paris fashions are mainly covered by dames," he said. "The dames have their names on the chairs. But everybody tries to get better seats. They fight and scream and call each other names."

The Balmain showing seemed to be for buyers. They were a seedy-looking bunch, considering the gaudy goods they were looking at.

"Also spies," said the Balmain lady next to me.

"Spying on what?"

"On the line. They sketch, then they rush home and copy."

The buyers also fought for chairs. They moved around a lot. Entrance was by ticket. The chairs had names on them for reservations but nobody paid any attention.

The showing was for 2:30 but did not actually get underway until 3. It lasted until 4:30 and a dress was shown every 20 seconds. The dresses were worn by eight models, all about five foot eight. They were built straight up and down and hadn't an extra pound on them.

There were 184 dresses in the collection. Also three new perfumes.

Not knowing much about haute couture, I did not take notes on the clothes. But I sniffed each model as she passed. Unfortunately I had a slight cold. But they looked like they smelled good, you know what I mean?

"The straight line has been resolutely stripped of all superfluous ornaments," said the Balmain lady. "Waistlines are normally marked. A natural bustline."

"You mean that scoundrel Dior is not going to upset the female figure again?" I said.

"The Balmain line favors the natural figure. In the suits we have normal basques. Not too short and rather close-fitting, often presenting a horizontal cut on the hips."

A model walked in with a sheath evening gown in canary yellow. A competent medic could have told you at a glance whether she had ever had her appendix out.

"What do you call that?" I said.

"Beside the pageant of grande robes, a very important place has been reserved for sheaths treated in plain, printed or embroidered silks. Ermine white, canary yellow and French navy dominate the collection.

"They are worn with jackets, with ample coats or with regally embroidered stoles.

"In the afternoon dresses, the décolletés become immense. They are treated flatly en accolade or lightly draped around the shoulders and bodice.

"The skirts are clinging or swollen in flat fullness."

"How do you swell flatly?"

"It is a Balmain trick of design. The straight line, softened with harmony for the spring days."

"What about hats?" I said. "I notice that many ladies pay much attention to hats."

"The hats are worn at an angle three-quarters to the back. They are either very important or careless shapes of casquettes or berets."

"You mean some hats are unimportant?"

"Only to the costume. All hats are important. Like this number here with the feather in it. It compliments but is not important in a design sense.

"The suit is one of a series of striped classic suits bringing

22

back to the memory Claude Debussy on the beach at Étretat. You recall?"

"Not exactly," I said. "A piano player wasn't he? Like Liberace?"

". . . after they've seen Paree"

From what I have heard, Paris was a mighty wicked city at one time. But that is all over now.

Frenchmen do not go around hollering "ooh-la-la." Like they do in the musical comedies. Nor do they pinch ladies. French mesdemoiselles do not swarm over visiting firemen. Reeking of that scent that drives men berserk.

I wore my fireman's badge one evening to test this out.

It was evening on the Rue Caumartin. Paris, city of romance. The lady slithered up to me like a tiger.

"Monsieur is lonely?" she said softly.

"Why, no, ma'am," I said, startled that a representative of the tourist bureau should be abroad so late. "But I have often wished for a pen pal. You see," I said, honestly, "I collect foreign stamps."

Nothing came of it, however. She never wrote. But possibly she lost the address.

Anyway, the only reason I mention it, is to report that tourists may visit France safely. There seems to be a lot of misinformation on the subject.

A good deal of this began after the First World War. There was a song, "How You Gonna Keep 'Em Down on the Farm, After They've Seen Paree?" I suppose Mr. Irving Berlin wrote it, because Mr. Berlin was writing nearly everything.

This seemed like such a good question I drove down through

23

France. To see how the Frenchmen kept them down on the farm.

France is full of farms. When I drove south from Angoulême, they were holding a fair in a little town called Chalais.

All the farmers had come off the farm. They stood around and pinched cows. There were dozens and dozens of cows in Chalais. Everybody was selling cows to each other.

The rain was coming down by the bucket. Nobody seemed to mind. They all carried umbrellas. There were some very pretty ladies checking the action on the open-air calico counters. But the gentlemen paid them no attention. All they did was stand around and admire the pretty cows.

Obviously, this is how they keep them down on the farm. Who wants to go to Paris? No cows.

"Everything arranges itself"

To my ten-year-old daughter, Europe arranges itself in a pattern of dramatics. The hotel at Angoulême is "the place where you said don't go near the balcony because it might break, remember?"

The Black Forest is "where we saw the lady with the goiter" —a true red-letter day. Choupana in Lisbon is where we met the bullfight lady. There is the place where we played jacks and the place "where Father fell down the stairs." A most embarrassing reminder.

The road from Frankfurt to Paris is "where the man slapped that other man with the flowers."

It was raining all along N-3. The invasion route—Metz, Châlons-sur-Marne, Verdun.

To me, France is made up completely of bicycle racers, and huge tricorn ash trays with a black "Martini" on a red target. The bicycle racers were out in force. They were racing toward Châlons-sur-Marne. In all the French towns, the gendarmes were spruced up in white belts and white gloves. They directed traffic with that sweeping hand-to-the-heart gesture. All the people stood on the side and watched the racers go by.

The racers were dressed in colored shorts and T-shirts. They wore a sort of leather crash helmet. They pumped and gasped, up and down the green hills of France.

Each man had a pair of trainers who followed alongside on green Italian scooters. They shouted advice, which, as near as I could tell was, "Faster! Faster!"

Motorcycle cops preceded the racers and waved us off the road.

It was a Sunday and in the French towns, little girls in white Communion laces stopped to see the race go by.

The Paris-Frankfurt road runs through the flat wheat country of France. Through World War I names: Château Thierry and Soissons and Bar-le-Duc.

It is rather uninteresting country. Except for the pretty Marne villages. At Poincy I stopped in the Hostellerie du Moulin de Poincy for friande de veau, a veal slice in fresh cream and Burgundy sauce.

Near Meaux, another bike race was in progress. They were racing us this time. Cops halted me in the middle of the main street as the race concluded before a little stand where the Mayor and his functionaries stood beneath dripping umbrellas.

It was a close race. Green Shirt and Yellow Shirt came wheeling in with their trainers batting them on from the rear.

The Mayor descended from the reviewing stand with a

pretty French girl. She carried a big bouquet of red roses. He made a little speech and awarded the race to Yellow Shirt.

Green Shirt and his handlers let out great howls of protest. Green Shirt began clutching the air with one hand. Like a subway rider reaching for the strap on a rough road bed.

"Thief! Brigand!" yelled Green Shirt.

The Mayor calmly took the roses from the Queen of the Day. He slapped Green Shirt across the face with the roses. Rose petals flew all over the wet street.

Green Shirt staggered back three paces dramatically. His handlers seized him and carried him off.

The Mayor handed the roses back to the Queen of the Day. She handed them on to Yellow Shirt. She threw her arms around his neck and kissed him.

Green Shirt shook his fist. "Fascist!" he shouted.

The cops who had been standing by seized me as a routine incident to get things back to normal again.

"Alors, let's go," said the cop irritably. You can't arrest a Mayor for assault with roses. But you can always bawl out a motorist.

"Robbery," I said. "An outrage. It was Green Shirt by a kilometer!"

"Now, now," said the cop soothingly. "Tout s'arrange. Everything arranges itself. Beat it."

Meaux is sometimes known to us as "the place where Daddy talked back to the policeman."

Morning at Arles

I awoke early in the Hotel du Forum in Arles in the south of France. The big French windows were open to the street and there was a scattered burst of motorcycle popping from the Place du Forum.

"Pierre says don't forget the bread," shouted a woman.

"Pierre is a bum," said a man's voice. "Nuts to him."

The motorcycle engine caught and began to roar. It popped off and faded away around the narrow stone-walled streets of the Caesars.

Arles was a Roman town in Provence. Great chunks of Roman walls and truimphant arches stand among the entry ports.

The Place du Forum is like a stage set.

It is a tiny square with eight great elms. In the center stands a green bronze statue of a man in frock coat and pointed beard. He looks a little like the statues you see in sleepy Virginia towns of Robert E. Lee.

I went down and had breakfast beneath the green-and-white striped awning. On the terrace that is really the uncurbed sidewalk.

The waiter brought coffee and hot milk and croissants.

"A brisk morning," he said. Did I like Arles? Had I tried the Arles sausage, made with donkey meat?

Ludwig Bemelmans had made a portrait of the square. Had I seen it? I had indeed.

The Place du Forum was made for the artist. Or a one-act play.

The Hôtel Nord Pinus stands at the head. It is painted in peeling gray. At one end, a piece of stone building stands alone, sending a flying buttress flying into nothing.

The hotel help is out, washing down the sidewalks. A girl on a bicycle rides by towing a basket filled with unwrapped loaves of long French bread.

Across the street at the Bar du Forum, the mustached manager wheels his bicycle out of the bar and props it up beside the candy stripe uprights of the red-and-white awning.

Madame arrives to open the Tabac. Its red marking cylinder shows it has a French license to sell tobacco. She sets up two tables on the sidewalk flanking the doors. Like doll furniture.

Across a narrow alley is the balcony Restaurante Vaccares, marked in white on powder blue. Up the street, "Mon Bar" is a tiny entryway in pale green and tan. The Societée Lyonnaise shows a solid bankers' gold-and-black front on the corner. And beside my hotel is the gray Librairie Papeterie du Forum.

From time to time, people enter from the side streets. Like actors walking on stage.

A pastel green Italian scooter pop-pops across the Square and fades into silence behind stone walls.

In the Hôtel du Forum, Madame and her family are having breakfast. Their dining room is behind the hotel counter. If you have business with the hotel, you look over the registration desk directly into this intimate morning scene.

The mailman comes across the square. Dressed in khakis and a black and red pillbox cap.

The coiffeur shop opens for business by tossing a pail of water into the street. A light breeze rustles through the tall elms. A complete little life goes on in the Forum, walled off by centuries of gray stone.

A bicycle wheeled around the corner. A man in a beret got off with three long sticks of bread.

"Tell that bum Pierre I got the bread," he said walking off stage down the alley.

Up a little narrow street, the hotel porter slid open a wooden door beneath an ancient building and pushed my little gray Simca down in front of the hotel. Somebody was practicing piano in the rooms above him. And the golden Provence sun filtered down on the Roman square.

ITALY

The feast of San Antonio de Padua was on. And in the warm, velvet Roman night, the people of Trastevere sat at tables on the cobblestones. Drinking red wine and eating the blessed bread and the enormous country mushrooms.

The little squares were full of accordion players. Out each window, the householders hung little lamps in honor of their favorite saint.

Trastevere—it means across the Tiber—is a workingmen's section. A section of narrow cobbled streets and Renaissance buildings that seem to lean over you.

In the garden of Romolo's we ate chicken cooked in green peppers and drank light ruby Broglio. A guitar player sang, leaning up against the broken Roman wall.

The grapevine that spread over us was 400 years old. Rafael's mistress lived here. Here in the garden where he painted her.

Twinkle, twinkle, little star

Miss Ioni Guerrina made her professional debut last night at the Trattoria La Villetta in Rome. She was a smash hit and remember, I said it first.

La Villetta doesn't get the carriage trade. It is a working-man's restaurant. In the Trastevere section, where sagging fifteenth-century houses sit on Roman foundation stones, and a little cobbled alley frames the lovely square of Santa Maria in Trastevere.

There is hard bread and chianti on the table and the audience is exacting. For more than an hour, Miss Guerrina had them on their feet and cheering.

It was a little family party in a corner under the brick arches in La Villetta. It was grandma's birthday. They had a guitar player and mandolin player and the waiters ran in and out with flasks of red chianti.

It was grandma who asked Ioni to sing.

She started out shyly, a music full of minors from North Africa.

"A complaint of the South," said the waiter.

You couldn't tell much about her voice yet. But it was true and there was a great gush of personality—that show-business quality that fills a small restaurant or a Hollywood Bowl.

It jumped across to you and all over the restaurant, people stopped eating and crowded under the arches to watch.

There was a little space between the tables. When the song ended she danced. Not so professionally but full of grace and fire. She had the sure touch to pull two bobby pins from her black hair and let it go. She had a smooth Italian face and complexion and her eyes were like black Italian olives in oil.

When she finished the whole restaurant broke down. Me, too. And Irving Hoffman, who has reviewed Broadway shows for some 25 years, clapped harder than I did.

Ioni came over and gave me her autograph in block capitals.

I O N I   G U E R
R I N A

Ioni Guerrina. She let the RINA come over on the next line. Because there wasn't enough room and it is hard to write small when you are only ten years old.

When the music stopped she was just a little girl again. In a brown and yellow sweater. I asked her where she learned to dance.

She said she "just learned. In the street, from the people."

"Do you see it in movies? Do you go to movies?"

"We used to go when I was little," she said wistfully. "But now mama has a new baby and we don't go."

"But you learned some things."

"All my life I wanted to dance and sing. Sometimes I see people dancing on the television. I stand in the street before the bars and watch through the doors. But most of the time they just talk."

She said her father was a tailor who worked at home in the Trastevere section. After a while she sang the "Song of Rome" and danced a bolero number with an absolute touch on the rhythm.

Well, it was a fine opening for a youthful artist and I am sure there will be a day when I will be proud that I saw Ioni Guerrina in her first performance.

"And do people feed cats anywhere else in Italy?"

"No. Only in Rome. In the Pantheon, the Colosseum and the Piazza Vittorio. Sometimes in the smaller forums there are cats to be fed. Here in the Pantheon it is an old, old custom. Until two hundred years ago, the Pantheon was a fish market. There were many cats."

"How many cats do you think there are now?"

"Who knows? Thousands and thousands. They belong to nobody. They belong to Rome. They came back after the war. Nobody knows from where."

The cats on the ancient pavement under the ancient pillars crouched like hundreds of small Sphinxes in the moonlight. They looked at us with calculating cat looks. Possibly they wondered how I would taste. Hunter style in red wine, oil and vinegar.

The long and short of it

The Trastevere section of Rome is the workingman's district. An ancient part of crumbling medieval buildings where candles burn beneath the Madonna over the door.

There are no sidewalks and the streets are cobbled. The restaurants are inexpensive. The food is excellent.

It has become chic among the elegant Via Veneto set to cross the Tiber and eat with the working classes. And Alfredo's in Trastevere and Cisterna are almost as crowded as Passetto's or Cappriccio's up on the hills of the rich.

I went over with Miss Gaby Lalonde, a French-Canadian journalist, who said Alfredo's and Cisterna were for tourists. Instead, she chose Garibaldina on Via Garibaldi. Near the Imperial gate where Roman countrymen brought their wine to be weighed and taxed as it entered the Eternal City.

And this is where I learned about spaghetti.

34

"This is spaghetti alla carbonari," said the owner. "It is the way the carbonari make it. The charcoal burners."

The carbonari are as old as Rome. They are itinerant workers, moving from place to place buying wood rights to lands.

"The spaghetti is put in boiling water with a little salt. This is important. If you put it in before the water boils, it cooks to mush. You boil it about ten minutes but it depends on the quality of the spaghetti.

"You should take out a piece and cut it on your finger. If it shows a little dot of white on the inside, let it boil more. Count to one hundred and it is done.

"Americans cook their spaghetti too long. They make it like rice. Spaghetti should be firm.

"While the spaghetti is cooking, you fry little pieces of bacon. You put this in a deep dish and beat up one egg for each person. Put the bacon with a little grease, a little oil, pepper and parmesan cheese with the eggs.

"Now lift out the spaghetti with two forks so that it drains lightly but doesn't stick together. Put the spaghetti in hot and stir it around. The spaghetti cooks the eggs as it is coated. Then serve it quickly."

It was excellent spaghetti and was served with white wine. Afterwards we went over to the square of Santa Maria in Trastevere where the washing hung out the upper windows of the antique buildings and a great fountain sent waterfalls into the clouded moonlight.

There is a little bar on the corner, next to Alfredo's, and we had the little half cups of black Italian coffee. An elderly lady came by picking up cigarette ends. Miss Lalonde asked her how it went.

"I am doing the misery," she said. Meaning she was doing life the hard way. We asked her to have coffee.

"Well, maybe I will," she said.

35

Miss Lalonde said the cigarette ends would be cut open. The tobacco would be mixed and rolled into cheap cigarettes to be sold one at a time.

After a while, some musicians came in for coffee. They said life in Italy was hard and poor. One musician was twenty-five. In a country where children go to work at eight, he had just managed to find his first job.

He worked as an ironmonger and his hands were rough and dirty and badly broken. He made a joke that he couldn't get a manicure.

But he was terribly ashamed of his talented musical hands. He held them together or put them in his pockets. And about midnight, we all shook hands and we went out to the car beside the fountain and drove through the narrow cobbled streets. Across the Tiber and back up the Roman hill where everybody has manicures and jobs and whole packages of fresh cigarettes.

Quick Watson, the needle!

The current medical bonanza sweeping Europe is akupunktur. An Old Chinese remedy of sticking gold and silver needles in you which, according to Peiping, does you a world of good.

The painter Picasso is being needled on the Côte d'Azur and the Aga Khan used to drop in for a light embroidery job at times. Among other things, the Chinese needle is supposed to flag the failing spirit. It works on aging gentlemen like catnip on a cat.

"It is very chic these days to be in tune with Peiping," I was told. "Leftist writers no longer go to Moscow. The bright light of revolution is in China. The Peiping ballet touring Europe is a social must.

"This attitude has slipped over into the medical field. And if you are ailing it is terribly old-fashioned to depend on any medicine but the Chinese needle."

I was sitting in the Excelsior bar in Rome the other night when Mr. Irving Hoffman, the Broadway raconteur, blew in from Munich. He said he had done three days of "akupunktur" and felt like a new man.

Mr. Anatole Litvak, the director, immediately sat up in his chair.

"I suffer from asthma myself," he said. He pulled a portable sprayer from his pocket to prove it. There is nothing like an exchange of symptoms to liven up a cocktail party.

"My needle doctor lives five flights up and the elevator doesn't work," said Mr. Hoffman. "Consequently he does not get people on their last legs, as you might say.

"He sits you down in his living room with all your clothes off and takes your pulse.

"Now the akupunktur doctor claims there is not just one pulse in the wrist but fourteen," said Mr. Hoffman. "He took my pulse and he said, 'You have back pains?'. . .

"Well, it is a fact that I have back pains as well as many other rare and complicated ailments," said Mr. Hoffman. "He then began to put in the needles."

He drew a little sketch to show how he had been needled. One in the head. Two in the forehead. In the shoulders, hips, hands, knees, and feet. All together, 19 needles.

"He leaves these needles in for about fifteen minutes. After that he put me on a couch. It so happened," said Mr. Hoffman, "that he left a couple of needles in my stomach. When I turned over, they nearly killed me."

"Do you bleed?" said Mr. Litvak shuddering.

"They only put it in a quarter of an inch," said Mr. Hoffman reassuringly. "No blood. You don't feel a thing."

"I'd rather have asthma," said Mr. Litvak gloomily. "What else?"

"They light a fire in a glass and clamp it on your back. It raises a suction. The needles have something to do with your meridians. Such as, if you have liver trouble, they might put a gold needle in your knee and a silver needle in your shoulder.

"These are the ends of the meridian line that crosses the liver. When the two needles get pulling at each other your liver gets so happy it flips."

"And how did you feel?" said Mr. Litvak.

"Sensational," said Mr. Hoffman. "When I got back to the hotel, I felt terrible. I went to sleep and woke up feeling great."

"It sounds like it might help my asthma," said Mr. Litvak thoughtfully. "Are you going back?"

"No," said Mr. Hoffman. "I'm going to Montecatini for the waters. Now there's a cure. Let me tell you about it . . ."

"The king and I . . ."

His Majesty, King Farouk, walked into Bulgari's jewelry store on the Via Condotti the other day. This news being reported by Mr. Irving Hoffman, the blade of Broadway, who advised me to dust over and see Miss Pat Rainey for further developments.

Miss Rainey was singing "Love for Sale" in the Kit Kat Club. She sang it as though love was going out of business and everybody should hurry.

"Would you mind telling me what the King does on the approaches?" I asked. "Are you expecting any baubles from Bulgari's?"

"Well," said Miss Rainey, "that cat is very astute. He knows human nature like mad. His approach to a girl in individualistic. It depends on the person entirely."

Miss Rainey said the King came into the Kit Kat Club when she arrived a few weeks ago.

"I was only in town a day and for me Rome was nowhere. I couldn't talk the language and was coming down with the flu. My back was toward the entrance and I didn't see him until a friend of mine took me over to be introduced.

"They just introduced me to the aide. So I just treated Farouk like somebody you hadn't been properly introduced to. You know, joe-blow-go-blow. I could see he was mad and pretty soon he stalked out.

"Next time he came in was Sunday. He sat there drinking orange juice—he doesn't drink, see? Well, I walked over and I said, 'Sire, do you remember me?' A friend of mine told me to call him sire," said Miss Rainey. "After all in his country he could have thrown a bomb at you and only send apologies to your respective governments.

"So he said, 'I certainly do, Miss Rainey.'

"I said, 'That's funny because we weren't introduced properly.'

"He said, 'I know and you did the right thing.'

"This cat knocks you right down," said Miss Rainey. "He said, 'I saw you in Paris and I liked you better when you sang at Ray Robinson's Ringside. What's that rat nest on your head?'

"Well, I had my hair cut too short and was wearing a switch. It was a blow to my ego. 'Oh,' I said to myself, 'a real sparring partner.' He said, 'I don't like your shoes either. They don't become your feet.'

"I said, 'Listen, they're Rayne's shoes same as Queen Elizabeth's.'

39

" 'Well, I don't like them,' he said.

"O.K. If I have two egos, he's deflated both of them, see? So we had a drink and after all these left-hand remarks he asked me if I was feeling peckish. Did I want to eat?

"So I said no, I was keeping my figure. 'It's well worth keeping,' he said to me. 'How do you get your weight down?' I said, throwing him a curve. 'I'm always like this,' he said. Well, he's dropped a lot of weight. I said to him, 'Now, sire! Just a minute! I saw your picture before!'

"I could see he was highly flattered," said Miss Rainey.

Miss Rainey showed me a cable from *Jet* magazine, asking for her life story with Farouk.

"Did he make any mention of jewelry or mink coats or anything?" I asked.

"Not directly. But it figures that a girl Farouk is interested in has got to do good. I didn't go out with him because that cat is always getting into hungs. He gets hung up in this and that mess and I didn't want to mess up my job.

"I saw him at another club later. He was with a blonde looked like a lady wrestler. I was with a couple of gentlemen from Egypt. Tobacco growers.

"The next time Farouk was in, he said, 'I see you been out with half of Egypt.' I said, 'Well, I thought I'd get the layout of the country.' He's got a great sense of humor.

"I always called him sir or sire and that completely disarmed him. At least I like to think so," said Miss Rainey. "After all maybe he never met an intelligent girl before."

For $16 I bought a bus ticket for three days, Rome to Nice, France.

The wayward bus

The CIAT bus came to pick me up in the morning at the Hotel Flora. All CIAT operations are hotel pickups. It is like having the Greyhound drive up to your front door.

It was an overcast morning. The sirocco was blowing in from the Mediterranean, whipping sheets of water over the Roman wall at the end of the Via Veneto. I paid my bill, tipped all around and, while my baggage went on the bus, took a taxi down to the Piazza Esedra. To sit beside the lovely fountain and have a farewell cappuccino while the bus made its pickups at other hotels.

CIAT runs on strict schedule. And at 8:15 we were off on the ancient Via Flaminia, where the paving stones of the Roman consular road run alongside the modern asphalt.

The stewardess was a pretty Italian girl in a French-blue uniform. She got on the loudspeaker and introduced herself. Then she introduced the pilot and co-pilot. The pilot was driving so he just raised himself in the seat a few inches and tipped his cap and dodged a taxi.

The co-pilot got up and made a deep, sweeping bow.

The bus to Florence was packed. The bus between Florence and Rome is always packed. As we drove along, the stewardess turned on the radio and, from time to time, gave commentary on the passing countryside.

She apologized for the weather. But actually it was very pretty driving through the rain.

The rain beat down on great turreted castles of the Middle Ages. On gray stone hill towns that rose above the water marks of a hundred invasions.

We passed farms where white oxen pulled harrows in the

rain and farm women were throwing powdered lime on the fields. The Lombardy poplars had turned a pure gold and the wet leaves blew over the highway. The grapevines had turned —some yellow, some deep red.

The CIAT bus bucketed down the Via Flaminia with its horn going ooh-ah, ooh-ah. The driver sat on the right, the co-pilot calling the passing shots from the left.

Along here, Caius Flaminius met Hannibal and was whupped. Caius then fell on his sword. As I point out to my daughter, this is what comes of running around with sharp things like scissors in your hand.

CIAT sold us lunch tickets for the hotel at Assisi. But when the bus stopped under the Roman arch, I saw a "ristorante" sign across the way. The proprietor was no fool. He had planted a pretty waitress in the doorway. She stood there with one hip out and her arms folded. An American tourist looked.

"I feel like eating in some place different," he said. "I'm tired of being regimented."

His wife took him by the arm and marched him up to the hotel.

As for me, I went over and had a piece of young kid, stuffed with garlic, some Gorgonzola and Chianti and coffee. I overtipped the pretty waitress.

With the rain coming down on the great church of St. Francis and the leaves blowing wet and cold on the steep old streets.

SPAIN

Every road in Spain is being done over. It is amazing for in all Spain I saw only two pieces of road machinery. The main highways are laid by hand. Like mosaic. There are gangs of men breaking big rock into little rock. The little rock is loaded in plaited straw baskets on the sides of burros.

Over on the road, tar is whirled by hand cranks over a wood fire. The tar is poured on the road. Rock goes in by hand. Oil goes over the top. A string of little boys walk up and toss sand on the tar. Eventually a machine comes in and lays concrete.

Everybody waves and cries "Adios" as you drive by. And during the siesta hour of the long afternoon, you see them in the shade of the cork oaks with goatskin flasks of the thin red wine of Andalucia.

"Rings faint the Spanish gun"

On the down grades, the little French Simca ran like a race horse. Sometimes 40 miles per hour. But on the uphill, it wheezed with asthma en rodage.

"En rodage" is French for "breaking in." For the first 300 miles the car must be run at low speeds. So that I would not cheat, the Simca people put a governor on the carburetor.

In the old university town of Salamanca, I completed my 300 and sought a garage. This meant switching my hard-won French garage vocabulary into Spanish.

"A little thing for make the car run slow," was the best I could do. The Spanish mechanics were entranced. It is not often in Salamanca that you get a chance to take a completely strange car apart.

The mechanic gave it a couple of thoughtful raps with a wrench. He got an assistant and began wrenching things off the inside. I could see it was an enormous job and went to lunch. There was a horrid clatter as something fell down inside the car.

Salamanca was an Iberian town. Hannibal stopped here three centuries B.C. to get his chariots repaired. The Romans built it into a city. During the Moorish occupation it lay on the high road to Portugal.

During the thirteenth century, the great Salamanca University was founded. From across the river, the university and

44

the great cathedrals are wonderfully imposing. Like a fortress town.

The Michelin guide recommended a restaurant in the Plaza Mayor. The restaurant was fair. It was filled with Spaniards hard at the afternoon work of drinking little cups of coffee and checking the action.

The action was out in the plaza. It was a flat concrete square, completely surrounded by old buildings that formed a wall. You enter through arched gates on foot.

Shoeshine boys hustled the customers. If you are not drinking coffee in the old Spanish tradition, you stand around and get your shoes shined.

The waiters had that frayed-cuff look that Spanish waiters seem to have. Spain is not a rich country. The hills are bare and the grass is cropped to stubble by sheep.

The waiter brought Paella Valenciana. This is a saffron rice dish, loaded with chunks of fish and chicken. With red pimientos sliced over the top. Lunch was six courses. It cost about 60 cents.

After lunch I went into a bookstore and asked for the most popular book in Spain.

"All these are popular," said the Spanish bookseller. The shelf was full of paper-backed pocket-size books. All of them were written by "M. Fernandez y Gonzalez."

I chose one called *Amores y Estocadas*. It looked like a *Forever Amber* thing. A lady in antique gown was reaching for a gentleman in knee breeches. It seemed it was part of a series.

"Don Francisco de Quevedo y Villegas has gathered glory with his poetic pen and overcoming difficulties. But in this novel, the author presents him with his loves and formidable sword."

The scene opened in Madrid in 1624 with a grinding of gates and a cry of "Come and get justice!"

45

Which reminded me of the grinding justice being done to my Simca.

I am never sure just how much to tip on first days in new countries. But I gave the boy watching my car about 10 cents. He shot off into the plaza with the look of a man about to buy a Cadillac.

"It was only this," said the mechanic holding up a little piece of wire. He said the wire was attached to the carburetor. The Simca, he said, would run fast now.

After I got 10 kilometers out of town, I found that it ran fast downhill. And slow uphill. In fact there was no change.

I never did find what wire he cut off the Simca. Or why the Simca people put it there. And since it would have taken much time to go back to Salamanca, I went on along the Iberian-Hannibal-Roman-Arab-Spanish road to Portugal.

La hora crítica

"No taxis," said the doorman at the Hotel Fénix peering up and down the street. "Es la hora crítica. The critical hour."

It was 9 o'clock in the evening. The cocktail hour in Spain. Up on the Gran Vía you can scarcely walk. It is crowded like Fifth Avenue on the lunch hour.

All Spanish hours are critical to me. The Spanish clock is not geared to American habits. When Spain is sleeping, I am working. When Madrid goes to bed, I am just getting up.

The Spanish businessman goes to work about 10:30 in the morning. At 1 o'clock, Madrid shuts up shop. They eat the big lunch and go home and sleep.

They reopen from 4 to 7. (Except in the summer when

46

Madrid works until 2 in the afternoon and then closes for the rest of the day.)

From 6 to 9, the night clubs open. Something like a tea dance. People who don't go to night clubs sit at the sidewalk cafés. They drink coffee and check the passing action.

Nine o'clock is the cocktail hour.

Dinner starts at 10 but most people eat about 11.

At midnight the night clubs open again. The first floor show is at 1:30 in the morning. Madrileños get home from 4 to 5 A.M. At 7 o'clock in the morning, the American tourists get up and wonder where everybody is.

The Gran Vía was packed with people at 9:30 in the evening. Gentlemen follow unaccompanied ladies down the street making romantic remarks.

The ladies walk along in pairs and threes. They pretend they do not hear these gallant statements. Everybody window-shops.

"This watch is an heirloom," he said sidling up to me and flashing it from under his coat. "Smuggled. Cheap. What is the best watch in the world—Patek Philippe. This is number two."

The watch had a white plastic band and glowed golden like a polished bar rail. It had dials to tell time, speed, dates. And what Golden Boy did in the fifth at Pimlico. In a box of Crackerjack, it would have been wonderful.

"I have a watch," I said. "In case I need to know la hora crítica."

"A Parker 51 fountain pen," he said whipping it out from an inner pocket. "Smuggled. Cheap."

"Made in Italy?" I asked curiously. Italy has a thriving factory that makes counterfeit Parker 51 pens for the tourist trade.

"In America," he said. "The best in the world."

47

At 11:30 I wandered over to the Casablanca. Madrid has a number of excellent night clubs and they are inexpensive by dollar standards.

The waiters thought I must have come in to collect a bill. The orchestra was just warming up. But promptly at midnight, the place began to fill. At 12:30 it was jammed.

A number of unaccompanied ladies came in. In Madrid this is part of the night club routine. The Casablanca had a dance floor with the orchestra on a stage. There was a balcony linked with tables and a bar upstairs.

The ladies without escorts stood around the bar. At times they would wander over and peer over my shoulder. They snapped their fingers. They did little time steps. They pulled their dresses as though they were adjusting a girdle. They were very animated and gave the impression they would be glad to sit down and discuss stamp collections.

At 1:15 I was so sleepy I called for the bill. Even the manager came over to see what was wrong.

"But the floor show is just starting," he protested. He presented me with a silhouette someone had clipped and pasted while I was not looking. It made me look 10 years younger.

"It is the equal of you," he said flatteringly. "Stay. Drink. Be gay. At three o'clock, another floor show."

"Toujours gai," I agreed. "The problem is, for me this is la hora crítica."

Madrid was jumping all around me as I drove home. It was exhausting just to see it.

Cooked in the ink

One of the favorite dishes of Spain is calamares en su tinta. Squid in its ink.

It seems the little octopus secretes an ink—a good deal like a journalist. And is often cooked in it—likewise.

A few years ago, Restaurante Los Calamares was just being discovered by the American tourists. And Mr. Santiago Armenez, the proprietor, shipped his son off to America to learn the trade.

"When he came back," said Mr. Armenez, "I was sure I had raised a maniac as a son. 'Papa,' he told me, 'we must change the place all around. We must put in atmosphere and insult the customers.'

"I said to him: 'Jorge, insult the customers? We shall soon lose all our business.' 'Just the Americanos, Papa,' he said. 'Watch me.'

"There were an American lady and gentleman in the restaurant. Jorge took the table himself. What did he do? The first thing he told them, 'We are all out of squid!' The specialty of the house."

"Why did he do that, Mr. Armenez?"

"Ah, exactly what I thought. They ordered red wine. He brought them white. He spilled a little on the table. He managed to put his elbow in the gentleman's face.

"At last he told them—what arrogance: 'Perhaps I can get you some calamares.' I tell you I was so nervous, I cooked the order myself. 'Calma, Papa,' he told me. 'I learned a great deal working in New York.'

"Finally toward the end of the meal, he became pleasant to them. He brought them the strawberries from Aranjuez. He suggested Carlos Primero brandy. He had learned to wait on tables all right.

"At the end of the dinner, he called in a guitar player from the street. Not good but fair enough. He shook hands with them at the door.

49

" 'But why, son?' I said. 'Papa,' he said, 'the Americanos must be given first the worst service. In this way they appreciate what you do for them last. Look.' He showed me the tip —an American ten dollars! About 2000 pesetas!

" 'Is it like that in New York, son?' I said.

" 'You cannot imagine, Papa,' he said. 'In New York I would have demanded a tip just to let them sit down at the table!' Is this true, señor?"

"It is true, Mr. Armenez."

"My son told me, 'In America there are 160,000,000 people. Of these, 2,000,000 live on tips. They hold the other 158,-000,000 in terror. In subjection like kings.'

"Since then," said Mr. Armenez, "Los Calamares has done better and better.

"Jorge has thrown out the silverware that cost me a fortune. We make the tourists eat with cheap wooden spoons. He sold our table linen—I hate to tell you what it cost me. We have flimsy checkerboard tablecloths.

"He trains the waiters himself. It is difficult to untrain a trained Spanish waiter. But we take only the most intelligent.

"They are trained to be difficult. Whatever the customer orders, he must look pained. As though they had made an order for ice cream on the squid.

"Jorge tells them: 'It is very simple. First, the tourist must feel that he is not a guest but an intruder. Second, he must feel that he has done something foolish. Thus, when you are nice to him toward the end, he is most grateful.'

"It has been an expensive education," said the proprietor. "But worth every peseta. Jorge has just finished a study in Paris. He says the Parisian waiter has learned the lesson well. But he says, 'Papa, nobody knows how to insult the customer like a New York waiter. They have a natural talent.'

50

"I intend to go to New York myself," said Mr. Armenez. "To see this wonderful thing. Such a land of opportunity! Every waiter a king."

The barber of Seville

Bullfighting, said the barber in the Hotel Fénix, had gone to pieces in the past few years. The bulls were poor. The matadors lacked skill. The picadors cut the bull to ribbons instead of pic-ing them properly.

Some of the toreros were using a plastic sword during the passes! They exchanged it for a steel sword just before the kill. The plastic sword was lighter.

"I am emotional about these things," said the barber stropping his razor. "I come from Seville. All Sevillanos are very emotional."

I didn't really need a barber. But what do you do when all Madrid goes to sleep in the afternoon? The hours drag and a barber is a good way to kill time between 4 and 5 o'clock.

"Only the great Manolete has been produced in the past twenty-five years," said the emotional barber starting over my face. "Señor, you should have seen him. The graceful butterfly pass. The larga cambiada de rodillas as the bull entered the ring. And what bulls! Like locomotives."

Bullfighting has become somewhat of a scandal in Spain recently.

A few years ago, 18 ranches paid $6000 in fines for sending undersized bulls into the ring.

Bulls were found with horns shaved down. The tips were painted black so they looked normal. Shaving the horn down is exactly like cutting a fingernail too close. After the bull has bumped this tender tip a little, he is more cautious.

"They hold the bull in the chute before the entry and drop sandbags on his back," groaned the barber with his emotional hand trembling over my throat. "Bang, bang. Over the kidneys, señor. It hurts the poor beast and he cannot turn swiftly.

"With others, they drain three liters of blood. He tires quickly. Scandalous."

Bullfight fans are never very happy. One year the bulls are no good. The next year the matadors are poor.

"I become emotional," said the barber scraping next to my ear. "A poor performance is not a novelty. They award the ear for nothing."

"Don't award yourself one of mine," I said flinching.

"Have no fear," said the barber of Seville. "With a razor I am like Manolete with the sword. Cold and determined."

Manolete was killed in Linares.

"The crowd demanded that he work closer and closer to the bull," said the barber slicing down the side of one cheek. "At last he had only one novelty to give. His life."

I said that if all toreros gave such a novelty, there would be very few bullfighters.

"True," sighed the barber. There will never be another like Manolete.

"But, señor, the pic-ing. Disgraceful. Spears like an ax. Chopping the animal into bits. The matador must prop him up for the kill."

The pic-ing is done by a picador. The picadors ride in with heavy leather skirts protecting their legs. The horse is padded with a blanket.

When the bull charges, the picador catches the force with a spear blade in the neck. The spear breaks down the neck

52

muscles. As the bull tires at the end, his head hangs low enough for the matador to stab him with the sword in just the right place.

"If today's matadors had their way, they would have spears like scythes," snorted the barber. "What they want in the spear is la bomba atomica."

The barber stood off and made a butterfly pass over my face with the towel.

"Yes, I go each Thursday and Sunday," he said. "Why? In hopes that some torero with a brave heart and steel nerves will appear before a bull of size and courage. I must go. I am a Sevillano and very emotional.

"But the old days are gone, señor. The scandalous tricks. Small bulls. Matadors with their eye on a safe life and a fat purse. The padded horses. The plastic swords.

"Why at the end one day, they did not drag the bull out with mules as is the custom. Señor, they dragged him out with a Pontiac station wagon! I was so emotional I could not cut hair for two days!"

Tourist prices

Caesar rebuilt the Iberian walls of Seville. The Moors laced it with arabesque, the Giralda tower and the Alcazar gardens. The Catholic Kings raised the cathedral, third largest in the world.

Over the narrow twisting streets floats a rich, ripe odor of the years. Olive oil. Garlicky gazpacho soup. Black coffee, burros, small dirty boys and old age.

The hackie of Seville sat asleep along the bank of horse carriages near the Andalucia Palace. His coat was frayed. But his battered uniform cap sat at a jaunty angle. He opened one eye and gave me the wise look of a New York taxi driver.

53

"Thirty pesetas an hour," he said. You could see his mind turning over silently: "God is good to the Sevillanos today. Look at this rich foreigner."

Well, 30 pesetas is only 75 cents American. "Let's go, Admiral," I said.

The tour was conducted in Spanish. It was flung generally over the shoulder and strained through a homemade cigarette.

We got three blocks to the Giralda tower. "A beautiful view," said the driver preparing to go to sleep again. "Climb, climb, climb to the top." The horse knew the route. He was already asleep.

"I have a defect of the heart," I said. "Possibly two months to live. None if I climb the Giralda tower. Let's go."

The driver turned and gave me a wary look. He drove on to the Alcazar. "Home of the Moorish kings," he said. "Beautiful, beautiful, beautiful."

"So I see through the archways," I said. "Andale. On your way."

As a matter of fact, no one should miss the Alcazar or the Giralda tower. But I had seen them once before. What I missed last time in Seville was Seville itself. The city.

Seville lies along the river Guadalquivir. The Betis, the Romans called it. You can see pieces of the wall that Caesar raised. The twisting streets come directly from the Moors. Like the river's name. Like the flamenco dancing and castanets and the wailing, quavering songs and the smooth, olive complexion.

Columbus sailed his ships down the Guadalquivir. Cortez came back to Seville to report the conquest of Mexico. Muleloads of Peruvian silver crossed the Andalucian plains with the Giralda tower as a guide post.

Alongside the Cathedral are the Archives of the Indies. A

block-square building around a patio. In thousands and thousands of leather volumes are the account books of 200 years of conquest and discovery.

The letters of Columbus under glass. Balboa writes of a great ocean across the Isthmus of Panama. Plans of fortifications at Cartagena. Reports of Indians with quills of gold along the Chagres. "In this land there is said to be a mighty Indian monarch whose subjects cover him each day with gold dust . . ."

Reports of fever. Reports of English fleets before Portobello. Morgan's scaling ladders in Cuba. Dutch guns in the Caribbean. Drake's pennant along the Spanish Main. Probably the most fascinating library in the world.

The driver stopped hopefully before a souvenir shop in the barrio Santa Cruz.

"A shawl," he said hopefully. "Castanets? Muy alegre. The spirit of the Sevillanas." He pulled one eye down with a forefinger that means: "Take a look!" "Are you kidding?" Or sometimes: "Catch the pretty girl."

"Let's go to the gypsy district," I said. The driver gave a long sigh and rapped the horse sharply with the reins for loafing.

"The cost is ninety pesetas," he said, when we finally returned to the hotel.

"Servicio extraordinario, no?" I said. "I see by the notice posted here in your carriage that the price is twelve pesetas per hour."

"Servicio turistico," said the driver. "You didn't tell me you wanted to ride."

Music, maestro, please

The best place to stay in Seville is at the Andalucia Palace. A true palace that belonged to Alfonso XIII. But at night you go across the street to see flamenco dancing in the Hotel María Cristina Bodega room.

I caught this stamping, castanet dance in the evening. And next afternoon I went down to the rehearsal. The dancing maestro is Enrique Gimenez. "El Cojo," the Lame. A little over five feet. A fat butterball of a man with one short leg.

The pretty Sevillana girls wore white, unpressed rehearsal dresses and were busy stretching each other's legs. They would hang on the bar rail. Two other girls would seize a leg and pull it straight up in the air.

"The Sevillanas have the aristocratic spirit," said El Cojo. "It is manifested in the soul of the city and in the dance. Muy poetico."

The piano and guitar started up and a girl named Margarita de Mayo came out and began to dance.

The flamenco dance is from the Moors who held Seville for 500 years. It is danced with the flounced, swirling skirt.

"It is my inspiration. Alégria en la calle. Happiness in the street. I listen to the music and I see the dance," said El Cojo.

He got up and began to correct the dancer. He danced with the girl following him. It was absolutely great. All the limp dropped away. You didn't see the unpressed pants or the fat man. Only the light, graceful dance.

El Cojo sat down again and said Margarita de Mayo had the makings of a great dancer.

El Cojo said he had been teaching for 18 years. He had taught so many he could not remember them all.

All the girls he teaches now are studying to be professionals. They get a little money from the Hotel María Cristina where they dance in the evening. It is a tremendous bargain for the hotel because this is really about the only place you can see it in Seville. Oddly enough, there is very little outlet once a girl has learned to dance.

"Then they must get a contract and go away," said El Cojo. "Here in Seville there is no place to dance except for one's self."

The girls in the white rehearsal dresses went on stretching each other's legs as though a whole future depended on it.

Lunch for the lions

A few miles out of Seville are the ruins of Itálica. The Roman General Scipio built it for a rest camp in 208 b.c. He built a huge coliseum so the GIs could go down on Sundays and see some of the population eaten by lions.

This did not please the local luncheon club. Since they were the main course. But as the General remarked:

"What is good for General Scipio is good for the country."

Itálica thereafter grew into a town of 200,000 people.

Three Roman emperors were born in the city. Trajan, Hadrian and Theodosius.

There is a one-room museum among the olive groves at the end of a sunny dirt road. The head keeper said he did not care to walk up among the Roman streets as it was too hot. He sent a young boy in a straw hat who pointed out the main street, the main sewer and some fine mosaic floors that have been uncovered.

"And now we see the coliseum," said the head keeper when

we got back. It was pretty obvious this was what he was saving himself for.

You walk through Roman gates into corridors beneath the stands. In the center of the arena is a deep pit with columns. The Romans flooded the pit for miniature naval battles. When they wanted to cover it, they put beams across the columns and covered the whole thing with wood.

"Look down," said the keeper. "Below here, the cages of tigers, panthers and lions.

"Here in the arena los Cristianos.

"Below here, the ramp. The lions, tigers and panthers mounted to the arena. Y los comen! They ate them!"

He fell back two paces and looked at me triumphantly. Not every day do you see where they served Christians for a snack.

"How many?" I said.

"Thousands," said the keeper happily. "Thousands of Christians eaten by lions, tigers and panthers."

He was tremendously pleased. He said Itálica was one of the greatest Christian-eating arenas in the Roman world.

Itálica was famous for three things: It was the only Roman arena that was elliptical instead of round; it was third largest, ranking only behind Rome and Nîmes in France; it was famous for its cuisine of Christians.

He sounded off like a representative of the Chamber of Commerce. Not a Christian got away from him.

As a matter of fact, I believe he had developed the story somewhat. For Emperor Theodosius became a Christian himself. And the lions, tigers and panthers went on a restricted diet.

Little wine of the country

On a narrow Pyrenees road between a rock cliff and a rushing cold mountain stream there was a striped, barber-pole road block. A green uniformed Spanish Policía Armada leaned out the window. He said if I was going to Andorra would I wait a minute please. He was frying eggs over a roaring fireplace.

The feudal state of Andorra lies between France and Spain. It is administered by vote of its 6000 people and by representatives of the Spanish Bishops of Urgel and the French Counts of Foix.

The national pastime is smuggling.

I spent the night in Seo de Urgel on the Spanish side.

On the road up, a policeman stepped from a sentry box and asked for identification.

"Passports?" I said.

No, he did not want passports. He wanted "personal identification." It had to do with the Bishop's See of Urgel.

I selected the handsomest card in my pocket. It is a rich royal purple and gold affair. It says I may take martinis without hindrance in the Iron Horse in San Francisco. Signed, Don Keating, Public Relations Counsel.

The policeman looked at it with respect and waved me on my way.

The policeman at the Andorra frontier came out wiping egg from his mouth. He had buckled on his black suspender belt and pistol to make it official.

He said I could go to Andorra, certainly. But I could not go on to France.

"Muy alta," he said. "Snow on the passes."

Consequently, I drove back to Seo de Urgel. A mountain

meadow road runs north about 30 miles. You cross into France at a tiny border station.

It was sunny and warm and the road ran through banks of vermilion poppies. The Pyrenees snows were melting and rushing down to the sea.

At a turn in the road between the rock walls, there was a sign: *Thues-les-Bains.* A massive antique hotel rose three stories from rocky gardens and old stone steps. Brown and white pigeons were wheeling over the roof.

The lady owner came out. She said yes, she could prepare a special lunch of the Pyrenees and would I like to see the hot springs while waiting.

I was the only visitor in a great banquet hall. It must have been an elegant spa in the Eighties. The bottled water said it was good for nervousness. Also gout, afflictions of the lung, liver, and a boon to growing babies.

The "salad" was hot boiled potatoes and navy beans. The lady said you sprinkled this with olive oil, vinegar and salt. She brought in a plate of green olives and black salami. "Spécialité de la région."

A small steak in butter and garlic. Biscuit St. Paul, a sort of macaroon, and a white cream cheese that is eaten with sugar. She said the wine "Pipi d'Ange" was a specialty of the region too. And she gave me the little card attached to the bottle.

"In the times of the Kings of Majorque, the Sire of Ronas and his eight sons cultivated a noble wine on a hillside between the sea and mountain."

One by one, the sons were knocked off in war. The eighth son was too young but was carried off in his fifteenth year by "un mal mystérieux."

The Sire of Ronas said to himself: "What is the use of raising such a noble wine? All it does is make our men strong and courageous enough to be killed." He thereupon set fire to the works.

However, says the legend, the children of the country were nourished on this wonderful wine instead of on milk. For this reason, the countryfolk called it "Pipi d'Ange."

It was wonderful dry white wine. I looked up the name later in my pocket dictionary. And I was never so surprised in my life.

PORTUGAL

I can see why the European kings come to Lisbon. Since the climate is to a king's taste with the great Atlantic surf breaking on the beaches. And the prices to suit a king's purse. Especially if the king is no longer on the payroll.

If I were a king sitting it out, I think I too would come to Lisbon where the hills are green and topped with old castles of other kings. The sun is warm and the wine is mellow and the olives and almonds are sweet and salt. And sit about and think of times when the people cried "Long live the king." And I would be assured that in this kingly life I would not only live longer, but probably look younger too.

. . . A word for it

The Portuguese have a word: "Saudade." They could not get along without it. Saudade means sadness, happiness, homesickness, love. And, for all I know, television.

I crossed the Portugal border at a little sunny station high on the edge of the Spanish plateau. A soldier in a gray uniform and a dark blue pillbox cap came out of his house and let down a low chain. He said would I please stop in a little town one kilometer onward and check my passport. "Comprendo?"

It was evening in Guarda where I checked into a balcony room at the pleasant Hotel del Turismo.

All the young men were walking in the plaza. They wore flat black hats with the ribbon bow at the back. They wore black capes and looked like advertisements for Sandeman port wine. They were filled with "saudade."

"You want to marry the girl but her father will say no. You have saudade," the headwaiter explained.

"Suppose her father says yes?" I said.

"Also saudade, for happiness," he agreed.

I gather it is something like "Aloha." Or maybe "Mabuhay" in the Philippines, which means "love, hello, good-bye, hurray and victory."

In the morning, I went out on the balcony and listened to a fine blare of bugles and drums from the local garrison.

The road went down and down through pine trees. Beside rivers and through lovely whitewashed, red-roofed Portuguese towns. The ladies were very healthy and pretty. They walked barefoot on the highways with big water jugs on their heads.

Walking with a water jug gives them a hip swing like a hula dancer. It makes you feel quite saudade.

As we drove by, all the gentlemen on the road took off their hats. All the people not wearing hats or water jugs waved. The sides of the road were covered with wild violets. And where the pine trees stopped at the edge of the villages, they were replaced by olive trees. The sun got warmer and warmer and the road dropped down and down.

At the lower end of the road, we came into the university town of Coimbra. No town is more filled with saudade. In fact, the song, "April in Portugal," was written originally as "Coimbra."

Coimbra is a lesson
Of dreams and tradition
A teacher and a song
A moon with feeling
A book and a girl
Only passing who understand—learned and understand "Saudade."

All the students stood around the street in black frock coats and black ties and full-dress trousers. For a while I thought it must be a great restaurant town and all the waiters were on their way to work.

This is student tradition, however. Students wear this dress as a symbol that they are all equal. They live together in little fraternities called "repúblicas."

When a student likes a girl, he cuts a little piece off the edge of his black cape and pins it on her. Thus you can tell a popular student by the scalloped edges of his cape.

"But," said the waiter in the Hotel Astoria, "some of these boys in their rooms at night cut pieces off their capes. So everybody will think they are popular."

He recommended a fine Dão wine and a garoupa fish. Also a dish that was spelled something like "Saudade."

It turned out to be creamed spinach.

Coffee and a song

All day long (when they are not eating the long lunch), the Portuguese gentlemen belt the coffee.

There are coffeehouses for financial people and coffeehouses for bullfight fans. Intellectuals, politicos. Artists and press agents.

Coffee is served with variations. A small cup is a bica. With a glass of water it becomes a carioca. With hot milk it is a garoto. Or in the large cup, a galão.

It is strong and black and heavy roast. The bica must be half full of sugar to drink.

Most of the coffeehouses are in the Praça Rocío, the beautiful central plaza of Lisbon. The "rolling square" they call it. Because of the rolling design of the mosaic inlay on the walks. Portugual gives the impression of being all tile.

In the evening, the gentlemen put aside their coffee and go to the fado spots. Best known are Machado's, Festa Brava and Faia Luso.

The Festa Brava is on a hillside of cobbled streets. The waitress suggested the sopa Alentejana. A cowboy soup with chunks of bread and "a whisper of garlic."

Apparently the cook thought I was hard of hearing. Bell-boys avoided me for days after.

We ordered a sangría—a wine and fruit juice mixture. The guitar players struck a few chords and a young lady stood up and began to sing a fado: "Roshina dos Limoes."

> He sits by his window and
> The world comes to life when she passes
> Her smile is full of promise
> Someday he will buy her lemons
> And later he will marry her.

The lady wore a black shawl. No fado can be sung by a lady unless she wears a black shawl. The fado has a Moorish quality. The voice takes a tone and lifts and drops it a half note.

It is sad as anything. As sad as "lonesome since you went away" songs in the States. The fado fans all sit around and are as hard to get along with as bop fans. If you so much as whisper, everybody hisses "sh, sh, sh."

After a while, Celeste Rodrigues came over. She owns Festa Brava and apparently is used to sopa Alentejana. She is the sister of Amalia, who sang in the States and is best known of women fado singers.

She said there are two types of fados.

"There is the Lisbon fado. Sung from the diaphragm. Dramatic and tragic. Like Carlos Ramos.

"Then there is the Coimbra fado. Like Felipe Pinto here. He sings from the throat. Very lyrical and romantic."

Felipe Pinto got up and sang a fado. Everybody said "sh, sh, sh." He gets $175 a month, which is considered pretty good in Portugal.

The fado seems to arise in the old quarter on the hill. Young fadistas tour the restaurants for meals, tips, maybe $10-$12 and a chance at the big time.

The fado "Coimbra" which became "April in Portugal" in the States is still café music in Lisbon.

It was written for a picture *Sale Touros* and starred the bullfighter Manuel Santos. This combination set a record by playing one Lisbon theatre for 19 weeks.

Marjane sang it in Monte Proser's "La Vie en Rose" in New York and started the composer off to $65,000 royalties.

Celeste Rodrigues introduced a new fado singer. She draped the black shawl on her personally for the send-off. We went back to our Alentejana soup and everybody said "sh, sh, sh."

I tried the "sh, sh, sh" for practice myself the next day at the Palacio Hotel. All the bellboys rushed to windward. Must have been something someone whispered to me.

Over the fence is out

There was rain lying over the warm Portugal coast. But they were holding a bullfight in the Praça de Alges. I had already spent $1.20 apiece for tickets for seats on the shady side. Which was a mistake as all sides were shady.

"Will they kill the bulls?" said the ten-year-old young lady who sat beside me.

"Indeed they will not," I cried. "And kindly say nothing about it. Journalists," I said, "who attend bullfights are sneered at by the public in America and often lose respect of the circulation.

"All of the bulls who have fought here are now retired. Happily married and living on pensions."

At this point they let in the first bull and everybody went over the fence.

The Portuguese bull ring is like the Spanish plaza de toros. A circular sand ring. Eight bulls are fought. Four on foot in Spanish style. Four on horseback with banderillas.

Our bullfight was a "festival." Everybody gets in the ring. This festival was held by amateurs of the school of veterinary medicine. One professional had been hired to cape the bulls off when they spilled somebody.

When the bull came in, the student on horseback raced toward him. He stuck him with a blue-and-white banderilla. A banderilla is a long stick of rosettes with a barb in the end.

The bull looked a good deal annoyed. He was black and medium size. His horns were in a leather padding. Like two glove fingers. The horse was a magnificent gray, trained for bullfighting.

The student took a pair of green-and-red banderillas and faced the bull again. He made a few passes and managed to get them both in.

The bugle blew for the next round and the horseman trotted out.

The second round of a Portuguese bullfight is most amazing. Four "forcados" come in the ring.

The forcados are on foot. They were dressed in red-and-gold embroidered jackets, lemon-yellow knee breeches and white stockings.

The cape men caped the bull and the forcados ran up behind him. They stood in single file. About two feet apart. The first man was about ten feet from the bull.

When the bull turns he finds the No. 1 man standing there with his stomach stuck out and his hands behind his back. The attitude says "butt me."

That is just what the bull does. He rams No. 1 man. Right in the Derby Kelly. The No. 1 man catches his arms around the horns. Nos. 2 and 3 men grab the bull by the horns. No. 4 grabs him by the tail.

When the bull is subdued, everybody lets go and runs for the fence.

The bugle blows. A door opens and four or five oxen come in with cowbells jangling. The bull joins up with them and they all run out. End of fight.

The fight on foot is more in Spanish style. The bull is caped around the ring. There is no picador on horseback to jab a spear in the bull's neck and weaken his neck muscles for the kill. The bullfighter comes in with a little red cape, the muleta. He has a sword to hold out the folds.

He makes his passes until the bull stands dominated with his head down. Then the bullfighter drops the sword. He makes a symbolic killing pass with his hand over the bull's neck.

The bugles blow. In come the oxen. End of fight.

Even so, it was quite a sight. With students being spilled in all directions. And everybody on the safe side of the barrera giving orders and advice.

Between times, the rain came down. Umbrellas blossomed in the stands and we ran out in the corridors to eat ham sandwiches and drink Portuguese wine.

"And nobody and no bulls were killed," I said to the young lady.

"Shucks," she said, biting into her sandwich. A bloodthirsty wench, that child. But remember, she said it. I didn't.

The night is young

At the elegant Palacio Hotel in Estoril: The Portugal sun comes through the balconied French windows early in the morning and the birds set up a respectfully subdued chatter in the date palms.

It looks a good deal like Santa Barbara, California. A layer of barbered parks and a layer of pink geraniums rise to white-washed, tile-roofed houses. The boulevard edges a crescent of Atlantic beach.

The sandboxes beside the elevators are freshly stenciled with blue sand: *Palacio, Estoril.*

This is the suburban home of ex-kings. The retreat of wealthy British refugees from socialized medicine. Assorted character types from the Levant and former international spies who lived here during the war on expense accounts.

The sun is warm, prices are low. The Portuguese escudo is hard currency and Dr. Oliveira Salazar has been firm in the political saddle these three decades.

In the morning, ex-royalty, British and American tourists head for the beaches.

They rent cabañas and towels from the beach boys. Men must wear tops. And women are allowed only one-piece bathing suits with a skirt in Portugal.

To enforce this, the Navy puts out a beach patrolman, the "cabo d'mar."

The beach boys in turn have hired a lookout. When the cabo d'mar is on the prowl, he comes screaming down the beach. Then royalty and tourists hustle into their cabañas. Or put on shirts and towels.

The fine is about $20. Like all fines in Portugal, it is collected then and there. You are given a receipt. Just like jay-walking in Lisbon which costs you 9 cents, paid on the spot to the cop.

In the late afternoon, the ladies hold teas in the highest fashion of silks and satins.

71

The cocktail hour starts about 7:30. The Palacio's bar and terrace are very fashionable.

"Over there, the richest Portuguese. At that table, a Belgian baron. She's a White Russian, the one with the bullfighter hat. That one was a German agent during the war, so they say."

The martinis are the best in Europe. They come in iced glasses crested with a blue-and-red *HP*.

The waiters snap cigarette lighters, licensed by the Government. All lighters are licensed, $1.50 a year. A $20 fine if you fail to do so.

About 10:30, dinner begins at the Estoril Casino up the street. There is dinner music and dinner for four with wines and brandies comes to $10.

You register to get in the gambling casino. No minors. No police nor military. No persons in the Finance Department of the Government or paymasters are allowed.

The inside is hushed like a public library. Long whippy rakes drag chips silently from the felt roulette tables. Coffee is served on little tables beside the players. A tiny bell like a dinner bell rings once in a while at the French bank table.

Any speech above a whisper draws a stare. The lowest chip is 18 cents. There is a bar. A few unescorted ladies can be persuaded to have a drink with you.

About 4 in the morning, the ex-captains and ex-kings depart. The sun edges over the date palms and the birds sing for them.

The lady and the bull

I had dinner at Choupana on the Lisbon coast with Miss Maria Krissie Tomara Louwe. Miss Tomara is a lady bullfighter. She is 25, stands 5 feet 6 inches, weighs 129 pounds, has green eyes and wears no girdle when fighting.

Talk about intimate reporting.

She said she could not be annoyed by a girdle in the arena.

"The bool turns quickly and I must turn quicker. Feel my arm," she demanded.

It seemed rather sudden. But I was afraid she would cape me around the table and stick me with a butter knife. For all I know she was without her girdle and could turn quicker than I could. I felt her arm.

"Muscle," said Miss Tomara. "Since I have fought bools, I wear a glove size larger."

The Choupana waiter swirled Constantino V. O. in warmed balloon glasses and the lights of Cascais glowed romantically up the coast.

"Yes, ma'am," I said weakly. Me and Miss Ava Gardner and bullfighters!

Miss Tomara said she could not be annoyed with girdles and she could not be annoyed with income tax.

"When I am in the arena I must think only of the bool."

The understanding Portuguese government therefore does not tax bullfighters very much. They make them fight benefits instead.

I asked Miss Tomara how she started to fight.

"I dreamed of a bool fighting," she said.

"A Maidenform dream?" I asked shyly.

"I dreamed of bool fighting so I went to bool fighting school," said Miss Tomara. "I paid 1200 escudos a month, about $42. I went to school for six months. Then I started taking lessons from the bool fighter, Domantino.

"Domantino has a rather cold style. But he is just my size and I could borrow his fighting clothes."

73

Miss Tomara is from British East Africa. She is a mixture of German, Greek and Dutch Afrikaans. Before she took up bullfighting, she was a model and a ballet dancer.

She fights in the Portuguese style and has never killed. They clip about two inches off the point of the horn here in Portugal. But they have no picadors to cut down the bull with the neck spear.

"This year I will kill in Spain and get my alternative," she said. "Then I must fight bigger bools. They are already big enough.

"I was fighting a monster this year. My assistant with the cape said: 'Where shall I place him, matadora?' I said: 'Take him somewhere where I can't see him!' "

She said she did not smoke or drink or eat fattening foods.

She wears the "Fato do Campero" costume.

"The Spanish 'traje de luz'—the 'suit of lights'—makes me look too fat."

The Fato do Campero is gray, high-waisted riding trousers and long-sleeved bolero jacket. It is worn with a white shirt and a flat black hat. The trousers come above the ankle, and split up the side and are worn with boots. You have to have the figure. Or a girdle. But it is very dashing.

Miss Tomara said she got between $2100 and $3500 per fight. Between times she has written a novel.

"About love and bools, of course. But the Portuguese publisher censored out the love scenes so I took it back. Maybe now I will give it to an English publisher."

She said lady bullfighters depended a lot on their looks. A North American girl "very good, very brave, got only 45,000 escudos. The manager told me: 'Oh, she is ugly.' "

Miss Tomara said she had an appointment with a government minister and was staving off an Army gentleman who wanted to marry her.

"But I don't want to marry. Only to be romantic."

She rose and caped me around the chair with her napkin. I turned, quick as a bull. But she was quicker. She was gone.

Pink pants and red wine

Before you get used to Portugal, you can become slightly confused. The scudo contains 100 centavos. And the $ sign is written in place of a decimal point. For instance there are 28$65 escudos to the U.S. $1.

We went into the local Stork Club in the fishing town of Nazaré. It was an open-air wineshop. Filled with barrels. A marble fountain stood in the corner for washing your hands.

Barefoot Portuguese moppets wandered in with raffia-covered wine bottles. The proprietor drew off the required amount in a funnel. He tucked the spout in the bottle and tripped a lever. The wine always filled the bottle exactly to the top.

It was like watching an expert bartender come out with a brimming measure on a martini.

The Portuguese fishermen stood around, belting the vinho tinto by the glass and, I imagine, complaining about the price of fish.

The fishermen all wore pink pants. They were in loud plaids, tied at the bottom so that they ballooned. Their shirts were plaids of violent contrast. Usually blues and purples. Around their middles they wound a black cummerbund. They wore long black stocking caps with their tobacco tucked in the end.

Not a man in the place wore shoes. They seemed happy, comfortable and full of wine.

While we drank wine with the fishermen, an American friend filled me in on some odd Portuguese customs.

"By some censorship which I have never figured out, certain moving pictures are open only to persons over eighteen. While others are open to persons over thirteen."

He said it made no sense by American standards. A picture with comedians like Dean Martin and Jerry Lewis might be restricted to eighteen-year-olds. And a torrid story that barely cleared the Production Code would be O.K.'d for the lollipop set.

He said it was even more odd when you considered that shady ladies are Government-licensed in Portugal. With licensing starting at thirteen.

"Actually it is a minor problem in Portugal and there is very little such going on," he said. "They did have a little trouble out at the Estoril Casino."

The Estoril gambling casino is the evening hangout for ex-kings and expensive visiting firemen. He said this proved very attractive to a good many imported Spanish ladies.

"In fact it got so that the ladies outnumbered the customers."

The management decided to discourage this influx of gaiety by putting a 100$00 escudo tax on all entries.

"It was very difficult. Because the management never admitted the existence of such ladies. Therefore they could not tax them directly. So they taxed everybody.

"Well, what happened was the ladies paid the tax without any fuss. But the customers rebelled. They just didn't come. So now the tax is off and everything is back where it started."

The Portuguese fishermen raised their glasses to us. We all raised our glasses back.

The sun poured through the open doorway off the narrow

streets of Nazaré. The Portuguese youngsters kept streaming in to fill the family wine bottles.

The price of fish was fairly low. But so was the price of wine. The high-prowed fishing boats were stacked on the beach, looking just as they did in the days of the Phoenicians. Everybody not drinking red wine was flaked out on the brown fishing nets. All splashes of pink pants and red and green shirts against the mahogany nets and the blue Atlantic.

April in Portugal

Well, April in Portugal brought the showers, which brought the flowers that bloom in May. Just as the song predicted.

After serious research, I find that love flourishes here just like everywhere else. Only with different ground rules.

Boy does not meet girl at dances. For there are no dances. A boy must follow the young lady discreetly to her home. He then sends a servant to her servant.

The servants have a glass of wine together.

"Nice weather we are having," says the boy's servant.

"So it was April in Portugal and now it is May. What's on your mind?" says the girl's lackey.

"Well," says the boy's man, "the kid in our household is troubled with saudade. Which, as you know, is another way of saying he is mighty young and sentimental. He is that way about your dolly."

"For a couple of escudos I could leave the window open," says the other.

"Boys will be boys," says the young man's man. "Have another belt of the vinho."

The window is left open so the young lady can hear. The young man gets a couple of guitar players under the window in the evening.

They tune up with a fado and the young lady listens. Sometimes she flings a rose.

"But," says my source, "he is never invited into the house until their parents meet and arrange a marriage."

It is rough on love in Portugal.

Mr. do Monte is a Portuguese gentleman of middle age and substance. A family marriage was arranged for him in his youth. It cut off his hopes for a lady of not so much family but closer to his heart.

Mr. do Monte made the dutiful marriage. In the European fashion, he set up housekeeping also with the other lady. This is understood and tolerated.

"A couple of months ago, Mr. do Monte took the lady to New York," said Mr. Ray Kohler, sales manager here for TWA. "He bought round-trip tickets."

Everything sailed smoothly until Mr. do Monte booked his passage home. The TWA man at New York airport noticed that he had a lower double berth.

"But the lady is not your wife," he said.

"I never said she was my wife," said Mr. do Monte amazed. He reached for his English translation. "She's my girl friend."

"But you can't do that," said the shocked TWA man. "Not on TWA."

"I just did on TWA from Lisbon," Mr. do Monte pointed out. "What's the matter with you? The lady and I have lived together for twenty-five years. Are you crazy?"

The TWA people went into a huddle. Mr. do Monte got madder and madder.

"You should have brought your wife," said the TWA man gloomily.

"You don't ship bananas to Madeira," said Mr. do Monte.

This Portuguese "coals to Newcastle" did not improve the situation.

Mr. do Monte suggested that he would not retire until the plane left the United States. The TWA man said what if the plane had engine trouble and had to return? Mr. do Monte said it was a poor way to run an airline. He bought another berth.

"When he came to see me, he was steaming," said Mr. Kohler. "Well, I gave him his fifty dollars back. What can you do? You have to understand these things. It was insulting."

Mr. Kohler was contemplating this when Mr. do Monte popped his head back in the door.

"I got even with that bum in New York," he said triumphantly. "I didn't use that berth anyway."

In all directions

The most elegant way to travel in Portugal is to stay in the pousadas. These inns are run by the Government. They are very clean and inexpensive.

The pousada at Obidos is in a castle in a walled Moorish town. You turn off the road at Caldas da Rainha—Hot Springs of the Queen. The town got its name in a curious way.

The Queen was very fond of poor people. She used to smuggle food out of the Palace under her dress. The King developed a slow burn in the matter.

"Madam," he said, "what happened to all the butter?"

"Butter?" said the Queen. "Why I imagine it is eaten up what with one thing and another."

"In that case," said the King, "I will have a peek at what you are hiding beneath the hem there."

79

But when the Queen lifted the hem, the butter had miraculously disappeared.

Obidos has a background of Kings, too. A Portuguese King took it from the Moors and gave it to his Queen.

The town lies completely within walls, with archery ports and the baffle gates of the Moors. The pousada is in the towered castle at one end of the long street, so narrow that the little French Simca barely slips through.

The odd thing about Portuguese pousadas is that nobody ever seems to be there. Only an old Portuguese woman was in the walled courtyard. She was blowing up charcoal fire in a big antique iron and obviously getting ready to iron the wash.

Pousadas seem to close up between 1 and 5 o'clock.

At the pousada near Elvas on the Spanish frontier, I found a bellboy asleep in the kitchen.

He found me a room overlooking the garden. He woke up a maid and went back to sleep again. The maid hoisted my luggage on her back and carted it up to the room.

After a little while I rang for a bottle of water. By this time the help had discovered there was a crazy Norte Americano in the house. Upsetting the siesta hour. They all disappeared.

About 5 o'clock I drove up to the city of Elvas.

"If you reach a pousada, eat. No matter what time it is," said Mr. Ray Kohler, the Lisbon TWA man.

Portugal is a wonderful country for tourists. But Portugal always seems surprised when any tourists show up. There are no restaurants and no hotels. There are no stores where you can buy food. At least I never found any.

I wandered all over the walled Moorish city of Elvas. Down narrow streets where horses were stabled in the front room. I found two shoeshops, a coffeehouse, a Chevrolet agency, a window full of watches and a harness shop with a shelf of thermos bottles.

I never found a food store beneath the Moorish arches.

When I got back to the pousada, the bellboy was up. All pousadas have a bar with four long-legged stools. I asked if I could have a martini.

"Certainly, senhor," said the boy.

He carried the keys to the liquor closet himself. He unlocked it and filled a wineglass. Half warm gin and half warm vermouth. He set it in front of me. It was a difficult situation for a person with no Portuguese.

"Son," I said, "you are probably gazing on the greatest martini mixer within a thousand miles. Now that you are wide awake, I intend to instruct you in the chemical arts."

We went into the kitchen together and got out the ice and lemon peel. And shortly thereafter I constructed a martini. The recipe was handed down to me by a grateful Indian chief. And I reveal it only in Portugal.

In the morning, the bellboy had not recovered enough to rise. I carried my own bags down to the car.

ENGLAND

Ah, London town. With your smoking chimney pots and great stone buildings. The Household Regiments parading in brass buttons and brilliant uniforms. The little square black taxis. The polished doormen. Afternoon tea at Fortnum & Mason. Pubs with English names: Crown & Anchor, the Jolly Ploughman, the Four Kings, the Rose & Thorn . . .

Stompin' at the Savoy

The Savoy Hotel is to London what the Waldorf-Astoria is to New York. Or the Palace to San Francisco. Where other great names have faded with the brownstone, these are the hotels with the vintage on the label.

The Savoy is a favorite of the more dashing American film people. (The quieter type stay at Claridge's or the Connaught.) Miss Ava Gardner rests here between bullfighting emotions. And it was here that Victor Mature went into a huff and flew to New York because his British hosts had not provided a shower.

It was quite historical to begin with. And Hollywood is adding an era all its own.

The Savoy has not straightened out the American accent yet. This is an even deal. I haven't straightened out the British. I pressed the buzzer marked MAID.

"Can I get some socks washed?" I said.

"I'm new here, sir," she said. "But wouldn't you rawthuh have them done by the cleaners?"

"I don't think so," I said. "This is a new idea?"

"I nevah hud of washing them, sir."

"I nevah hud of dry cleaning them," I said. "Just slosh them around in some soap." I got them out of my suitcase.

"Oh," she said, "you mean sawks. I thought you said slecks. Trousuhs, you know."

I ask you. Slecks, sawks? I called the operator. I asked for the press office. But the voice that came on answered "Room sahvice." So I went down to the press office myself. I was afraid the management would send somebody up to brainwash me if I didn't straighten out.

On information from Jean Gilbert, the prettiest press agent in London, I find the Savoy is built on the site of a palace. "The fayrest manor in Europe," they called it.

Henry III gave the real estate to Peter of Savoy. In the quaint English rental, Peter was to "yield yearly at the Exchequer, three barbed arrows."

Rents have risen considerably since then.

The palace then fell into ruinous conditions and nothing much happened until they built the hotel in 1889.

Lily Langtry lived here for 50 pounds a year. For 20 pounds more she got maid and hairdresser service.

The press book of those days gives quite a picture of the elegant life. The hotel had an unheard-of 70 bathrooms! Mature would have died in those days. It had hydraulic lifts—elevators, kids. Whistler, the man who did the famous picture of his mama, rolled out a canvas called "Savoy Scaffolding."

In 1890, Sarah Bernhardt came back after playing *Joan of Arc* and took too many sleeping pills. She was revived. The Duc d'Orleans came to dinner in a wheel chair, having fractured his knee. He was wheeled in by the Princess of Wales.

William K. Vanderbilt offered so much money to Chef M. Joseph that he lured him to America. Mr. Vanderbilt ordered corned beef and cabbage. Whereupon Joseph suggested he order dinner from the gardener and stalked back to the Savoy. It was a wonderful era.

The clippings are full of such material and it gives you an idea why this is still the plush name in hotels in Europe. Naturally, there have been improvements since popeyed reporters of 1890 wrote of the 70 bathrooms and "a plentiful supply of electric bells."

All the rooms have bathrooms now. And every bathroom has an ivory telephone. Take a bath. Call up your friends. Have a ball.

"He had his old school tie on"

"Sometimes I awsk meself 'Wot's the world coming to?'" said the London cab driver.

"Blime, guv'nor, you ain't just a-whistlin' Dixie," I said. For I speak English like a native when I want to. Also I had just left a fashionable pub called "The Coal Hole" where the warm beer made me ask myself the same question.

Beer is warm in England. Also it does not seem to be our beer. If you want our beer, you call for " 'arf a pint of bitter." It still comes warm. But it is recognizable.

"It's these Edwardians," sighed the driver. "With their wild ways and their velvet collars and drainpipe trousers. 'Orrible."

" 'Orrible," I said. "What's an Edwardian?"

The present-day shocker of London is a fashionable bully boy who congregates around the Elephant and Castle and the South Bank of the Thames.

The Edwardian dresses in royal blue or emerald green with velvet-faced collar and cuffs. The jacket is finger-length and has six buttons.

The trousers are well described as "drainpipes."

A "Slim Jim" tie, five feet in length with a tiny knot, is

86

part of the fashion. The shoes have thick crepe soles and patent leather toes.

"And I thinks to meself, 'Now clothing is orf the ration and this is what England has come to,'" said the driver. "The American films is what does it. You're American, I take it?"

"Canadian," I said.

"A glorious part of the Commonwealth," said the cab driver. "I should hesitate to say it if you were American. The films must bear the charge in the matter. Every lad is trying to look like Bob Mitchum or Burt Lancaster."

The Edwardian is uniformed from top to toe and from the skin out. His hairdresser spends several hours getting his locks oiled into styles known as "The Crew," "The D.A.," "The Burt Lancaster" or "The Tony Curtis."

His weskit must be of slightly contrasting color to the suit. And his cuff links, shot out from the velvet cuffs, proclaim the district. Classy emeralds to plain glass.

The "Slim Jim" tie is scrubbed until it shrinks into a piece of tape.

"Enough to make a tinker weep," said the cab driver.

Fashionable London shops in Savile Row. The Edwardians play the tailors of Clapham Common. In between lie the great London stores beloved of the tourist.

A good deal of posh is put out by British shops in the matter of guineas, pounds and pence. If you are buying a normal item, it is apt to be listed as so many pounds.

But if it is a luxury item, it is in guineas. A guinea being a pound and a shilling but carrying a very snooty attitude about it.

Personally I have never bought anything listed in guineas. But I have a charge account at Simpson's in Piccadilly. Where I can walk around the corner and eat at Wheeler's oyster house. Located in Apple Tree Yard at Duke of York Street. This being about as snobbish an address as you can use in casual conversation.

" 'Ardly a day goes by," said the cab driver, "but you 'ear of some going on with the Edwardians. The Dancing Boys and the Barrow Boys and Guards Officers and sons of Dukes and Barons. I blime it on the films," said the cab driver severely. "They should be taken in charge they should. Which I say, you being Canadian and part of the Commonwealth."

"Righto," I said. "And drop me off at the Crown and Anchor for a 'arf pint of bitter. It's been a dry year this year in Canada."

The old school tie

London's unpredictable weather has been blowing hot and cold again. Cold one day, sweltering the next.

This makes little difference to the English. An Englishman dresses by the calendar rather than by the weather. Easter marks the beginning of spring. And though it may be snowing in the streets, out come the bicycle riders in shorts.

The businessman on the commuter special leaves off his Burberry and appears in starched collar. Oxford gray pinstripes, bowler hat and furled umbrella.

His only concession to color is the Tie.

The shop windows are filled with the most startling spring apparel. Blue velvet hunting caps. Gray toppers. Tweed caps. Yellow corduroy caps. Caps in violent plaids.

I could not tell you who wears them. For I have never seen them on trains, streets or the big red double-deck buses.

The Tie is another matter.

I had lunch the other day at the Royal Air Club with Mr. E. A. Chris Wren. Mr. Wren wears the blue tie with tiny golden, red-crowned propellers of the club.

"The Tie," said Mr. Wren, "is the Englishman's method of swank in a sort of left-handed way.

"The Old School Tie has been expanded to the Regimental Tie, the Squadron Tie, the Tie for Men Who Were Shot Down in the Channel. The golden caterpillars of the Caterpillar Club who bailed out of planes. And so on.

"The English are very reticent. If an Englishman speaks to you on the train, he usually mentions the weather.

"Now with all The Ties, it makes a great conversational gambit.

"Somebody speaks to you. He says: 'By the way, old boy, what is that tie you're wearing? The *Daily Mail* Abominable Snowman Expedition?'

"You say, modestly of course: 'No, chappie, the Daily Twenty Club. For the chaps who splashed 20 Huns a day. Jolly place and rather good food, what?' "

'ow to jug a 'are

I checked out of the Calverley Hotel, where Queen Victoria and Albert stayed in Tunbridge Wells, and drove north to London. I drove right over to Rule's in Maiden Lane.

"The jugged hare?" I asked the waiter.

"Ah, sir, it's not on the menu, sir."

"The mating season?" I said knowingly.

"The myting season, sir," said the waiter.

I have an odd relationship with Rule's. The restaurant, just off the Strand, is about 500 years old. It is full of wonderful old prints and cast-iron cupids about to loose cast-iron arrows. The waiters are elderly and filled with tradition. The wine list is filled with vintage authority.

A specialty at Rule's is the jugged hare. Unfortunately, the hares are not co-operative. There seems to be some rule at Rule's against jugging a hare when he is baying the moon.

Though I have been in Rule's many times, I have only been able to get hare twice. Most of the time the hare has his mind on love instead of on business. To wit, the jug.

"I had hare just a month ago," I said. "Do you mean to say the hares have gone back to playing the ukulele already?"

"It's 'ard to say about 'ares," said the waiter. "Now the best time for jugged 'are is in early fall. The first cold snap. It quiets them down, you might s'y. Might I suggest the Dover sole?"

Rule's is always sawing off Dover sole on me. The Dover sole, I gather, is a clod. No romance.

We settled for lamb chops and the wine steward dusted off a half bottle of Rhine wine.

I asked if the manager was in. I had his name in my notebook.

The director is as elusive as the jugged 'are. He had written me a letter. He said would I please call on him next time I was in London.

"The director, sir? Why 'e's sitting at the bar."

"Will you give him my card?"

The waiter disappeared behind a cast-iron cupid and held a long conference. He came back to say the director was no longer at the bar.

"'E stepped out for a bit, sir. Probably for a bit of fresh air."

"Will you let him know I'm here? He sent me a letter asking me to see him."

"Yes, sir. May I ask the subject of your inquiry?"

"You may. I write for American newspapers. Once I wrote about Rule's. The director sent me a letter. He asked me to call."

"Ah, yes, sir. You wish to write about Rule's."

"I do not wish to write about Rule's. I may write about Rule's and I may write about jugged 'are. I really don't care to write. I just wanted to be a good sport and answer the man's letter."

"Yes, sir. You wish to answer the letter. You wish paper and pencil, sir?"

I said that was not the idea. Just tell the director I was around. If anything happened it would be all right. How about the Stilton cheese?

"Sorry sir. The Stilton is gone."

He went out for another conference. He came back to say there was *Cheddar*, sir, with port wine. Also—

"The director 'as gone down to Sussex for the weekend."

I said it really didn't matter. The 'ares and the director were hard to come by. But no doubt worth it when you caught them.

Never a fainting fit

Why don't they put subtitles on British pictures? So you can tell what the British actors have to say? As Mr. Joe E. Lewis is wont to remark during the course of the show.

Thus to Mr. Denny and the Slough Car Hire Service.

Ordinarily I rent my cars from Europcars. But being in the heart of Merrie England, I made my approach to Mr. Denny in Slough.

He turned out to be a cautious little man. Seated on a swivel chair carefully covered with a newspaper. Mr. Denny and I had come to serious regrets the day before. Regrets that I was a poor insurance risk because my international driving permit had expired a few days before. I came back therefore with a five-shilling British license. At 9 in the brisk Berkshire morning.

"I just 'ave a few cars and I do 'ope you'll be careful," said Mr. Denny. He did not sound very hopeful.

I told Mr. Denny I seldom moved out of a 10-mile gait. He sighed and began to fill out papers. Insurance papers.

I swore that I never suffered from fainting fits, weak eyes and had never so much as parked next to a fireplug. I paid Mr. Denny 12 pounds 6 plus a 10-pound deposit.

"I do 'ope you'll be careful," said Mr. Denny. "And now I'll show you the car."

"Mr. Denny," I said, "I'm anxious to be up and away. I really know a good deal about cars."

"Ah, yes, American cars," said Mr. Denny. "Not the Austin 40.

"Now 'ere is the snap for the bonnet," said Mr. Denny lifting the hood. "Easy does it. Never force anything."

Mr. Denny lifted out the oil gauge, ran inside and wiped it and dipped it in again.

"Proper and full," he said. "Always replace the dipstick carefully. Never force anything."

"And now I'll be on my way," I said briskly.

"And now I'll show you the rest of the car," said Mr. Denny unheeding.

Mr. Denny showed me the car. He showed me the starter, oddly enough marked STARTER. He showed me the choke. He showed me the lights. And 'ow you put them up and down by pressing the "dipper" with your foot, my lad. He showed me

92

the spare tire and the jack and something called "plays" or "place." I did not interrupt Mr. Denny. I was afraid he would blow his lines. And start over again.

"Drive carefully," pleaded Mr. Denny. "I do 'ope you'll be careful."

He advised me to keep petrol in the tank and air in the tires. With a little encouragement he would have come along with me.

"And now I'll go," I said.

"Now we'll put in some Red X. I don't know if you 'ave it in America," said Mr. Denny. "Lovely stuff. But expensive."

He rushed into the garage and poured off a fifth of some red oily material. He put this in the oil. He lifted out the dipstick. He wiped the dipstick. He showed me the dipstick. He replaced the dipstick. Carefully, without forcing.

He poured another fifth and unlocked the gas tank. Poured in Red X. He showed me how to lock the gas tank and assured me it was locked.

"And now I'll place it in position," said Mr. Denny.

He showed me all over again. The "H" shift. The choke. The starter. The lights. He patted the wheel and looked ready to cry. He showed me how pretty it was and pointed out the "cubby locker"—the glove compartment. He started it reluctantly and pointed it toward the street.

"I do 'ope you'll be careful," said Mr. Denny.

I moved behind the wheel and slid it toward the street. Somehow the gears meshed together like concrete mixing. A drip grind.

But it was too late to stop. I was already in the frightening British left-hand drive. I caught one last flash of Mr. Denny. He had his head in both hands and looked extremely faint.

Snowballs in July

Housing continues to be a problem along the Thames. Hardly a day but the newspapers recount how someone is being moved because they have too much room.

With all such space problems, the British hang doggedly to the tradition of odd rents.

The other day (St. John the Baptist's Day), a number of estates paid their annual quitrent of one red rose.

This summer, as usual, an estate in Yorkshire must furnish one snowball.

If Queen Elizabeth visits the Channel Islands, the Seigneur of Rozel must ride into the sea until the water reaches his saddle girths. He must act as Royal Butler while she is there.

There are rents to be paid in a pound of pepper for an estate in Sussex. The Lord of East Charlton pays the Queen 100 herrings on behalf of the town of Yarmouth.

There are two antique ceremonies in London Law Courts in October. The City Solicitor must bring a billhook and hatchet and chop two faggots of wood.

The Queen's Remembrancer then says: "Good service." And takes the billhook and hatchet.

The quitrent for a property in London known as "The Forge" is six horseshoes and 61 nails. All to be counted out for the Queen's Remembrancer who must remember, among other things, where he put the nails and horseshoes last year. They have been used for 500 years.

This June 18, the Duke of Wellington put up a new tricolor of France in the Guard Room at Windsor Castle. If he gets caught in a traffic jam and fails to replace last year's before

94

noon, he forfeits the estate of Strathfieldsaye, Berkshire. The estate was a present to the Duke who whopped Napoleon at Waterloo. But the new flag was the condition.

The Duke of Marlborough replaces a fleur-de-lis flag on the same day, same time, same station. This keeps Blenheim Palace in the family where it has been since the old Duke won at Blenheim in 1702.

The Duke of Buccleuch receives pennies to two shillings and threepence for rights to move cattle across his land. The tenants gather round a hollow stone on Martinmas. They fling the money in the stone saying: "Wroth Silver."

Anybody who fails to pay must be fined 20 shillings per penny. Or else a white bull with red nose and red ears.

After the ceremony, everybody goes down to the Dun Cow Inn at Stratton-on-Dunsmoor and drinks the Duke's health in rum and milk.

A new owner of an estate in Essex must ride to the Rectory. He takes his wife, a manservant, a maid servant, a hawk and a hound. He blows three blasts on his horn.

The Rector then gets up. He gives the owner a chicken for his hawk, a peck of oats for the horse, and a loaf of bread for the hound (who probably would prefer Red Heart).

The owner then rides off blowing three more blasts on the horn and annoying the neighbors.

The unruffled diner

While I love England, I must say that greater love hath no tourist than he take a knife and fork to English dinner. With some rare exceptions, the British fodder is fairly dismal.

I have heard a London taxi driver go into a drool over "roly poly puddin'." "You takes a bit of suet and wraps it in flour and bacon, sir. And you boils it 'arf an hour."

The roast beef of Old England is back after the long austerity. But it has not caught up with its American cousin from Kansas City.

It is my opinion that when Lord Nelson signaled the Fleet "Well Done," he was commenting on the prime ribs rather than naval tactics.

Nonetheless, he who loves England must eat. And the other night I went to the Elizabethan Room at the Gore Hotel in Queen's Gate. To see how they did it in the days of Good Queen Bess.

The Elizabethan Room is authentic from soup to pewter. It is a wonderful, paneled room with high arched ceilings. There are rushes on the floor and a warm fireplace.

The antique tables are set in a T. I imagine in Elizabeth's day, the face cards sat at the top of the T. The varlets sat along the sides and flung bones to the dogs.

There were two ladies in what waitresses wore in those days. The attire being attractive with a cleavage that would never get by the Motion Picture Code.

The lady explained that the whole menu was faithfully copied out of old cookbooks. Being divided in two parts—the first remove and the second remove.

It was as charming a dining room as you could find anywhere.

But I will report sadly that the ruffled Elizabethans did not eat any better than the unruffled British diner of today.

"I think you'll like the mead," said the lady. "It's made with distilled honey and apple juice."

I can get along without mead. One thing the Scots did for the English was to give them something fit to swallow.

Mead is served with the first remove. Along with it goes soup in wooden bowls. We all drank our soup from the bowls. Just like Sir Walter Raleigh.

There was also boar's head, some chopped peacock, cucumbers in Madeira wine and a thing called salamagundy which seemed largely horseradish.

During this remove, a lute player came in and began to sing.

He sang about a cabin boy who offered to sink the enemy down to the bottom of the sea. He was promised the captain's daughter. But later the old man welshed on the bet.

The second remove began with Good King Henry which turned out to be spinach. There was also champ which was some kind of vegetable in butter. Likewise fish and wild duck.

The payoff was artichoke pie with gooseberries. Surprisingly enough, it is better than it sounds. Though a long way from New England mince.

Along with this came hot spiced claret. And the whole thing finished off with tobacco in clay pipes and a box of snuff.

It was Elizabethan in everything except the napkins, the lady said.

"We do let you have a napkin."

I gather that in the old days, you wiped your hands on your pants. Or a nearby dog. Or possibly on a convenient lute player or waitress. I imagine it would be almost impossible to hire lute players or waitresses today under these conditions.

The nudge for this peek into England's culinary past is about $5. And possibly worth it to see why there'll always be an England. Only the hardy survived.

How to raise a cat

Bray is mainly noted for a line of verse:

"I'll still be Vicar of Bray, sir."

Though I have not checked this out yet. I have a very clever excuse. I have run into a situation about cats. Cats, I find, are on the British Government payroll. I have been investigating this as a fine thing for the U.S. Since we have got nearly everything else on the Government payroll. Why not a cat or two?

Cats have been on the payroll since 1868, when they started off at a wage scale of fourpence a week. For milk and such supplies as cats require.

The cats were hired by the post office. Particularly by the head of the money order department. It seemed that mice were eating up money orders and this is bad for bookkeeping.

He thereupon hurried over to his superior and declared:

"Let us hire a few cats."

Cats have been on the post-office payroll ever since.

I do not suppose this would have come to anyone's attention. Except for the editors of *Civil Service Opinion*. These fearless journalists found a sorry state of affairs.

Cats have had no pay raise since 1873.

There are other serious discrepancies.

From a starter of fourpence, cats were gradually raised to a shilling. Until in 1873, the London rate went to a shilling and a sixpence. Or about enough to get a small thanks if handed over as a taxicab tip.

Cats went through wars and depressions. Devaluation of the pound and inflation. Nothing!

Civil Service Opinion also regards sternly that Manchester cats have been frozen at a much lower rate than London cats. Only a shilling if you mouse around in Manchester.

Whatever happened to Harold

In my salad days, a good deal of education was sawed off on me. And among other items I recall King Harold and the Duke of Normandy making a big fuss hereabouts in Southern England in 1066.

So the other day I got in the little right-hand-drive Austin and drove down the left side of the road to Hastings. To see whatever happened to Harold.

It was a gray cold morning in Sussex. I took the little narrow back roads where the hedgerows rose on either side and the rolling hills were brown with frost-killed bracken.

It was damp and overcast. Blue smoke rose from the chimney pots above the brick farmhouses. The big farm horses stood snorting steam under the bare trees. Once in a while overhead you could hear the whistle of a jet barreling through the cloud.

In October of 1066, King Harold marched down this way. He did not march back, having been stuck with a very sharp arrow. The Normans then took over.

On the signposts, a good many arrows pointed to "Battle." This sounded likely so I drove over. Sure enough, this was where the whole rumble took place. Not at Hastings at all.

There are about three blocks of main street. Of "green-grocers" and "chemists" and "tobacconists" in Battle. I dropped into a sagging tearoom where the beam ceilings almost brushed your head and a fine cheerful little fire was burning on the hearth.

The waitress said yuss indeed, sir, this was where King Harold got the arrow. Up on the rise where the great Abbey towers like a fortress.

"They 'ad a 'orrible fight," she said, "and they do say it was a gory sight. Did you read about the lady lost on the Common, sir?"

I did read about the lady. She had been staying at a hotel in Tunbridge Wells. She had not come home to dinner. And now the police were out poking through the fernlike brown bracken.

"She's a goner," said the waitress gloomily. " 'Oo knows what 'orrible fate 'as 'appened to 'er. Walking about lonely like in the near dark."

"Do they know who shot the arrow into Harold?"

"Likely it was murder," said the waitress, "and they'll be hacking about in the bracken and come upon the poor corpse."

It was obvious she was only interested in modern history.

After I got warmed up, I walked up by the Abbey which has fallen into some disrepair. The Abbey was built by William the Conqueror to mark his victory.

The buildings and estate were sold after the Reformation and the last Abbot put a curse on the new owners. So many future owners died by fire and water (the condition of the curse) that in quite recent times the place was exorcised by the Dean of Battle.

Battle Abbey in the unruined part is now a school for girls.

There was a gatekeeper in a great coat and muffler with a red nose peeping out. And I asked him whatever happened to Harold.

"Now, sir, they're all asking that. The folk who come to see

Battle Abbey. Struck in the eye, 'e was. Struck by a Norman arrow. And where 'e fell the monks built the great altar. 'Ave they found the woman lost on the Common at Tunbridge Wells?"

I said when I left the police were combing the bracken.

"Murder if you ask me," he said. "Ah, there's murderers about would look you in the eye, innocent as a lamb. And in the evening be out with their murdering ways."

"Did they ever find out who shot Harold?"

"It would be a Norman bowman. But which one I'd not know that. It was all undisciplined troops, don't you see. When the Norman troops broke, some of 'Arold's men pursued them, sir. Likely for the loot. And the others stood about congratulating themselves while the Normans turned and murdered them as pursued. We'd never 'ave stood for such things when I was in the Guards."

When I left he called after me that likely they'd never find the woman on the Common.

IRELAND

Ireland is a peaceful land of green fields and gray stone fences.

Here in July the rain has put a chill on the hotel. I asked the maid if I could have a peat fire.

"I'll bring a bit of turf now," she said. "But we'll have to look first is there a bird's nest in the chimbley."

For the love of McClafferty

Toward midnight the green runway lights of Shannon came up under the wing. You could see the broad silver band of the river in the moonlight.

We drove through the twisting Irish roads to Ennis, where Mr. Brendan O'Regan was waiting at the Old Ground Hotel. Mr. O'Regan said he had just been appointed chairman of the Irish Tourist Board.

"Ireland is yours," said Mr. O'Regan. "While you are waiting to take over the real estate, have an Irish coffee."

"All I want is a room in Dublin," I said. "In London I had scarce a place to lay my head, since it was Derby Week. In Paris it was the Grand Prix. Wherever I arrive, the horses are there before me."

"Think of something difficult," Mr. O'Regan urged. "Will you have a castle now? Or will you stay at the Royal Marine in Dun Laoghaire?"

"Can I?"

"McClafferty loves you."

"He does? Very few people love me. My dog puts on a great show. Especially at dinnertime. My daughter exhibits a certain dutiful affection on Father's Day. By the way, who is McClafferty?"

"Mr. McClafferty is the manager of the Royal Marine. You wrote a beautiful article about him."

"And he loves me?"

"He adores you," said Mr. O'Regan.

In the cool of the Irish morning I got up and drove to Dublin.

The drive is left-handed. But the road is direct and not too crowded. At the Five Lambs in Naas I stopped for tea.

"If you'll be going to Dublin," said the tea lady, "I hear it's dreadful crowded."

"I have a room booked," I said. "Mr. McClafferty loves me."

It was traffic hour in Dublin. I pushed the little Austin Cambridge through narrow King's Street to St. Stephen's Green. Backed out of a one-way street and got on the road to seaside Dun Laoghaire.

"Out with the bags," I told the porter at the stately old Royal Marine.

The lady at the desk looked a little harried.

"We have received Mr. O'Regan's signal," she said, showing me the telegram. "But we are completely booked."

"A horse race?"

"The Horse Breeders' Association in convention, sir."

"What about Mr. McClafferty?" I cried. "Mr. McClafferty adores me."

"Ah," said the lady, "we were that full we had to hire out the manager's suite. Mr. McClafferty has had to get rooms down at Ennis."

I got on the telephone. In O'Connell Street the Irish Tourist Board has offices for the help of stranded wayfarers.

The tourist gentleman said there were no rooms at the Shelbourne. No rooms at the Gresham. No rooms at the Russell or the Royal Hibernian.

"I can get you a grand room," he said, "at the Lucan Spa."

"Where is that?"

"A stone's throw," he said. "But the waters will be doing you good. And you'll live by the castle of the great Captain, Patrick Sarsfield."

I told the lady at the Royal Marine I had a room.

"If there's another," she said, "you might book it for Mr. McClafferty."

And in the late evening I drove ten miles back to Dublin. Then ten miles the other side of Dublin. And settled down to take the waters of Lucan. A little on the sulphur side. But wet.

Feather Matches

The Irish rain has been pouring down for the past three days. From the mouth of the Liffey to Galway Bay. A gray curtain soaking the snow-white sheep that cluster under ruined stone castles. A cloud of umbrellas in St. Stephen's Square.

Dublin has a clutter of parking attendants. It is probably the only city in the world without a parking problem.

The parking attendants are ragged but officious men. They wear a uniform cap and direct you—no matter where you park.

"A full lock to the right, gentleman. Now back you go and a full lock around left."

I was "full-locking" right and left in busy O'Connell Street when the gear shift broke. It waggled like a broken arm. The rain was coming down in buckets and we pushed it alongside a mid-street monument.

"Just tell the car hire people yer alongside Feather Matches," said the attendant.

I dodged through the splashing big green double-deck buses into the Aer Lingus office.

"I'm alongside Feather Matches," I said into the telephone.

"Who?"

"Feather Matches. The statue on O'Connell Street."

"You mean the Nelson column?"

"I do not. I mean Feather Matches. Don't you know your own Irish patriots?"

The Aer Lingus lady looked out the window where I was pointing.

"Father Mathews," she said.

"Father Mathew's statue," I said.

"Ah," said the car hire man with relief. "We'll be right down."

I went back and sat in the car. The parking man came back and looked expectant. I gave him a shilling.

"Who was Feather Matches?" I said.

"Feather Matches?" he said. "The holy man was against the drink. But he meant no great harm by it. The Feather spoke out against whiskey so they put him up in stone."

I left him the keys and went up to Brian's pub where I ran into Mr. Seamus Kelly, the journalist, and Mr. Aleck Crichton, the Jameson whiskey may.

"They're putting up stone statues against you," I said.

"What statues?"

"Feather Matches," I said.

"Who?"

"If you can't understand Irish, how can a poor foreigner get along?" I said. "Feather Matches is up in stone in O'Connell Street against what you hold in your hand."

Mr. Crichton said the deep Irish was indeed hard to understand. But once you got the knack of it, it was very poetic speech.

He said they had a way of picking rhyming words. And he told of a lady relative who was boating on the Shannon.

"The ghillie was a fine, polite old chap. When he got her seated, he hesitated a moment and then said: 'Beg pardon, yer honor, but there's the laste taste of yer drawers showin'.' "

The rain was still coming down and I caught a taxi.

"Where to?" said the driver.

"Feather Matches," I said. "Him that's up in stone in O'Connell Street."

And he drove me right to it. It takes a knack.

The Groaning Stone

"All that the Irish have from the English is the coinage," said the bartender in the back room of the Bailey. "And little enough of that."

The Bailey was a fine old Dublin restaurant. In Duke Street, not far from the stone quays of the Liffey. It had scrubbed tables and a peat fire and polished beer pumps. Upstairs, there were rooms of oil portraits and tables covered with Irish linen.

I said I would have my coffee downstairs in the long back room.

The bartender made me a Gaelic coffee. The black coffee in a glass with a nip of Irish whiskey and thick cream floated on the top. He spread out a handful of Irish coins.

"Now it's the same as the English do you see," he said, "with the half crown down to the farthing. But each piece has the Irish harp on the back and an Irish animal on the front.

"A horse to the half crown. The salmon to the two-shilling piece. The hare, the greyhound, the hen, pig and woodcock.

"We take the English money at the same value. But it's temporary."

"Ah, never trust the cruel Sassenach. As me grandmother O'Dooleyplane oft remarked," I said.

"In the main, it was English money caused Ireland's troubles," he said. "You'll remember it was Cromwell gave Ireland's lands away for the rents?"

"To hell or to Connacht," I quoted, sipping the Gaelic coffee.

"Until bold men like Parnell stood up in the Parliament," said the bartender. "As you can see on the wall."

The walls of the Bailey are plastered with Irish posters of defiant days.

HOLD THE RENTS
Who Are the Gaolers of Charles Stewart Parnell
and Michael Davitt
Not Mad Blackstone or Blundering Buckshot
BUT YOURSELVES, IRISHMEN!

Who are content to seek and accept paltry REDUCTIONS and to let the men who won them for you—aye, and who will win much more, if you will but follow them faithfully— ROT and DIE IN BRITISH DUNGEONS!

"Another of the Gaelic, if you please," I said. "And I will advise the Gael to have no further dealing with the Gall. But to meet them henceforth with the strong hand and the sword's edge. As me grandmother O'Dooleyplane often said."

"There were bold men in Ireland in the olden days," he said. "And many the King's son rode with a price on his head. Have you been to Tara?"

I had not been to Tara.

"The home of the ancient Kings. It was at Tara the O'Neills were crowned. In direct descent from Niall of the Nine Hostages who bought St. Patrick in the slave markets of Bristol to serve as a swineherd on the hills of Antrim.

"Now I would advise you to go and look on the Lia Fail. A coronation stone where the Kings sat with their harpers around them. You'll remember the Stone of Scone underneath the English Coronation Chair in Westminster Abbey?

"The English believe to this day it is the true Coronation Stone. But surely, it is only a piece of ordinary field stone.

"The Irish gave them a bit of smooth tongue and a piece of rock that the sheep wandered over. The true Lia Fail sits as always on the hill of Tara waiting for a High King of Ireland to rise again.

"And if you doubt my word," said the bartender, "it is well known as the Groaning Stone. For the Coronation Stone utters a mournful groan when the rightful King sits upon it.

"You saw the English Coronation on television? Now let me ask you, did you hear a single groan? Well, then."

A lady's wish

A gray curtain of rain was still beating down on Ireland when I drove out of Dublin. Between showers, the road to Galway was lined with small boys and girls, selling mushrooms picked fresh from the fields alongside the great, gray ruined castles.

I drove through the late twilight to Cong where a window-less abbey stands on the edge of the village. Behind it rose the crenelated towers of Ashford Castle. A castle behind a moat. All dark in the upper windows with little flickers of candlelight appearing suddenly and suddenly snuffing out.

However, it was cheerful enough inside. There was a great fire crackling in the main room beneath the high ceiling of carved walnut. Fresh salmon and lobster on the table.

"And now I'll show you to your room, sir," said the hall porter after dinner.

"I'm not a bit tired," I said, peering down the dark corridor.

"Come, come," he said sternly. "A bit of rest will do you good. You're to be in the famous west wing."

"What's so famous about it?"

"Why," said the hall porter leading me into the gloom, "it's said, mind you, that the Fitzgerald of Amagh walks the halls of night."

"Can't he sleep?"

"The Fitzgerald of Amagh lived in olden times, sir. Tomorrow you should visit the cave where he stole away and had his will of nine fair maidens."

He led me up a flight of stairs and then down a flight of stairs. It was terribly dark.

"Why don't we go back to the bar and talk it over?" I said.

"It's only a twist and a turn further, sir. The Fitzgerald was known as Captain Webb. He stole away the poor nine maidens to his cave and at the end he pushed them over the brink into a deep hole."

"Why did he do that?"

"So as not to have the embarrassment of meeting them again, sir," said the porter. "I've brought you a bit of a book on the subject. Pleasant dreams."

There was no lock on the door. But I put a chair under the knob—so I would not have the embarrassment of meeting the hall porter again. Or anything else.

The wind was moaning outside the window and I did not feel sleepy at all. I felt like going back by the fire. That is how I felt.

The book said the Fitzgerald—him that was known as Captain Webb—promised the ladies he would take them to his castle. But with running out of gas and other excuses, they always wound up at the bottom of the cliff.

That is, until he stole away a fair maiden who, as the Captain put it, "You the tenth shall be."

The lady hemmed and hawed. She stalled around and said it was late and her family expected her to get in before midnight. And one thing and another.

She said the bushes would disarrange her hair. She practically wore Captain Webb out chopping down bushes. She then put him by the edge of the cliff and suggested that he look the other way. The book quotes:

> A lady's wish was a royal command
> To a gentleman like him.
> And as he spid
> To do what she bid,
> She pushed the poor lord in.

I figure a ghost who has been pushed in will only walk the first floors. Probably having a fear of heights. Even so, I slept lightly and crawled under the bed when I heard a ghostly knock.

But it was only the red-haired maid with the morning tea. And when she pulled back the drapes, it was a bright, sunny day. And I was as brave as the next man again.

"Oh, oysters come and walk with us"

In Galway, I dropped into O'Maille's shop in the fishermen's section and bought one of the thick-knit Aran Islands sweaters. It is worn bloused up with a narrow knit belt of many colors.

The shopkeeper said it was too bad I had not got around for the oyster festival.

"With all the sailormen dancing and singing. Though mostly now they're fishermen. But in the olden days we had great trade with Spain. There was a Galwayman now who sailed with Columbus, did you know that?"

I said I did not—until now. "What else do they do at the festival?"

"It is a beautiful ceremony. First comes the Lord Mayor in his fine robes. He eats the first oyster and takes a great drink of stout. Then me bold sailormen pitch into the thick of it.

"It is a fine time for all but Peter Greene, the Lord Mayor," said the shopkeeper. "For the poor man cannot abide oysters. And he loathes stout. But then, it's only once a year."

I drove down to Galway through the wonderful west country. A great empty land of low purple mountains and gray-green lakes. A road lined with fencing of green Connemara marble, and heavy clouds hanging over the peat bogs.

All along the roads, there were piles of dark brown bricks of peat drying out. There were fishermen on the rivers. For this is one of Ireland's greatest salmon runs.

Only sheep can live on the short grass. The whole gray-green landscape was dotted with white sheep. (Irish sheep always look freshly laundered.)

They were marked with little splashes of red or blue dye—the owner's marking.

It is wonderful historic country. Near Cong is where the prehistoric invaders defeated the Firbolg—the original Irish.

The skyline offers a procession of stone castles and churches, most of them built by Turlough O'Conor, the King of Connaught.

"Have you been to the Corrib country?" said the man at O'Maille's.

"I drove through it this morning."

"It was the country of the bold O'Flahertys. When the Burkes and the Lynches, the Joyces and all of them held Connaught it was the O'Flahertys harried them. Above the west gate of the city, they put the sign: *From the fury of the O'Flahertys Good Lord deliver us.*

"Did the good Lord deliver them?"

"Ah, no," said the shopkeeper. "They were delivered by Cromwell. A black day for Ireland. To be delivered by the English and a Protestant on top of it all! It's enough," said the man at O'Maille's, "to make a man lose faith and may God forgive me for the saying of it.

"Now some say," said the shopkeeper, brightening, "that The O'Flaherty was undone by his own greed.

"If you passed opposite Lough Corrib at Maam Arm, you've seen Hen's Castle. The strong castle built by the sons of Roderic O'Conor.

"They say that The O'Flaherty was presented the castle by a witch who gave him in the same bargain a wonderful hen. A hen," said the shopkeeper, "would lay enough eggs for a whole garrison in time of siege.

"But eggs was not enough for the bold O'Flaherty. Nothing would do but he must have stewed chicken. So into the pot he pops the wonderful hen. And so he was soon starved out."

From Galway Bay the Irish road dips southward along the Atlantic coast through the barony of Burren. A land so bleak and wild that the Irish say:

> "No wood to hang,
> "No water to drown,
> "No earth to bury,
> "A man in Burren."

On this coast, the dying wrecks of the Spanish Armada went aground.

"The crews was kilt entirely by The O'Brien, the one was

114

Earl of Thomond," said the pub keeper at Lahinch. "Though a Clancy had a hand in it."

The mounded graves of the Spanish sailors are on the shore.

Gaelic coffee

If you drive south from Shannon Airport, you come to Kerry.

"The county of Kings. Ah, they're proud folk live in Kerry. With an accent you will not understand."

Which is true. I had not gone very far on the narrow, rainy roads of Kerry until I managed to slide the little car into a big, muddy ditch.

It was Sunday and far out in the country. A little band of sheep was working over the green rocky hills.

Several of them came over and looked at the car. But apparently they decided it was hopeless. For they made no effort to pull me out.

There was nothing for it but to leave the car on a muddy bias and hike to a farmhouse.

It was bitter cold. By and by a car came toward me. I flagged it down. There were three men headed for the next town. The car had no back seat and not much in the front. I sat on the floor.

They asked me how I liked the car I was driving.

"Is it fairim?"

"How's that?"

"Is it fairim? Is it sawleed on the road?"

I said it was both firm and solid. Except when it slid into a ditch.

Two of them went up the road and snipped a length of

barbed wire from a fence. They hooked it between the two cars. I gunned the motor and everybody pushed and the car ahead pulled.

It came out with a great sucking noise.

I asked the Kerry men if I could stand them a drink. They said no, it wasn't necessary. They were going up to Killarney for a nip of the Irish.

"We'll be back with the lambs."

The lambing season is beginning and foxes are killing the young lambs. It is a curious business.

In order to cut down the rabbit population, Ireland introduced a rabbit-killing disease. Myxamatosis.

The myxamatosis killed the rabbits all right. But it left the foxes with mightly little in the way of groceries.

The foxes thereupon turned around and began eating lamb chops.

This is what comes of fooling around with the lamb and peas. The rabbits no longer eat the farmer's peas. But the farmer is having a harder time getting lamb.

Down near Sneem on the southwest coast, they were whipping up a Sunday fox hunt.

The master of the hounds was standing in the street and from time to time he blew on a little brass horn bent into a circle.

The street was loaded with hounds. They did not appear very anxious to go hunting. They ran up and down the street, sniffing at trees and checking the local action.

They paid little attention to the horn. Two or three of them looked like they had hangovers. They sat near the man with the horn and their ears hung down in a most downcast look.

A couple of them went to sleep. I could imagine that a quick brown fox would jump over such lazy dogs. Especially being full of spring lamb chops.

The hunters had not appeared. But a few townspeople stood around and watched the dogs and listened to the mournful horn.

A few farmers were in town. They stood in front of the local pub and read a poster saying: *Next Sailings for America. Agents for Cunard Line.*

The Irish rain began to fall again. The foxhounds paid it no attention. They went on sniffing the town as though they had never been there before. The farmers went into the pub. And I climbed back in the muddy car and drove through the lonely Windy Gap over Killarney.

> Health and long life to you,
> Land without rent to you,
> A child every year to you,
> And may you die in Ireland.
> —Gaelic toast

"A chef by the name of Joe Sheridan invented Gaelic coffee," said the man at the Shannon Airport.

" 'Twas in the old days the flying boats were landing at Foynes. About '38 I should say. The passengers would come in by launch, shivering and shaking fit to die with the cold and all.

" 'Surely,' said Joe Sheridan, 'we must invent a stirrup cup for the poor souls, and them not able to put their shivering hands in their pockets for a shilling to pay unless we warm them.

" 'What is more warming,' said Joe Sheridan, 'than Irish whiskey, smooth as a maiden's kiss. To take the chill from their poor shaking hands,' said Joe, 'we will fill the glass with coffee, black as Cromwell's heart. We will top it off with a floating inch of Irish cream.'

117

"We have been serving Gaelic coffee since," said the Shannon airport man.

"And where is Joe Sheridan now?" I said.

"Ah," said the Shannon man, "Joe Sheridan went to Chicago to make his fortune. The last I heard, he was chef at the Chicago airport."

I asked him if he knew that Chicago's airport was dry. A technicality of state law since the school system owns the property.

"Poor Joe," sighed the airport man. "A cruel thing it is to go to America to become rich."

I told the airport man a story. Once I landed at Shannon with a prominent Bostonian and initiated him into Gaelic coffee. Later he told me he was an ardent Prohibitionist. I was afraid to confess the foundation of Irish whiskey. But he said it was the best coffee he ever had.

"More like a tonic it is," agreed the Shannon airport man. "Sad it must be for Joe Sheridan and him off in the far-off lands. Forbidden by the law to manufacture the angelic brew he invented in those shivering days at Foynes.

"A cruel law," said the airport man, "and it would surprise me none at all it was an Englishman thought it up."

THE NEW WORLD

CALIFORNIA

The aspen are turning gold up in the California Sierra. The creeks of the Mother Lode are down to a trickle, awaiting the winter rains.

In the crisp frosty mornings you can hear the flat crack of a deer rifle. And there is a welcome blaze in the fireplace when the sun drops down in the Sacramento Valley and the evening chill blows from the mountains.

My great-grandfather dug gold here:

"The gold mines of California was all the talk," he wrote in his diary. "And when you got the itch, brimstone and grease wouldn't cure you.

"On the third of September, 1850, after traveling overland all summer, I arrived at Weberville, a gold mining town 50 miles northeast of Sacramento City. I was out of provisions and 2500 miles from home; had a pick, a shovel, a frying pan, three blankets and a rifle."

"Hear that choo-choo blow . . ."

The Del Monte Express is a cozy little train running between Monterey and San Francisco. It leaves Monterey at 7:25 in the cool gray mornings, runs along the bay and out into the sun between the lettuce and artichoke fields, and along the still inlets where big white cranes walk on stilts and pick up a morning frog for breakfast.

Everybody knows everybody else on the Del Monte and coffee in the club car is like a family breakfast. It takes three hours to San Francisco.

In the afternoon at 4 o'clock, the Del Monte turns around and comes back. Loaded with the same passengers. The passengers loaded with packages. It is smooth, unhurried and comfortable.

I suspect a whole generation of small fry, hurrying into the age of the jet transport, may be missing something.

When I was a boy, the Del Monte was curtained and tasseled and had green plush seats with antimacassars.

All the BIG people rode down to the old, magnificent Hotel Del Monte. Presidents and bankers and stockbrokers. The ambition of every small boy was to be an engineer on the Del Monte. With a striped, peaked cap and a hand on the throttle and the lonely whistle blowing for the crossings.

122

I think the Del Monte these days is hauled by diesel. Anyway the whistle hasn't got that wonderful whooooo-whooooo sound any more. Just a horn blast like any truck.

The club car at that time was run by Mr. Oliver Millet who was the porter. He rode the Del Monte for 30 or 40 years. Up to San Francisco. Down to Monterey.

He served highballs to Secretaries of State and tea to ladies. Once I saw him give a couple of aspirin to Salvador Dali whose mustaches were drooping.

He knew all the mothers and fathers and all the children. When the children grew up, they brought their children on the Del Monte. Children were well behaved on the Del Monte because everybody got dressed up to go to the city.

After these 30 or 40 years with the Southern Pacific, Oliver was retired. The Southern Pacific bought a big new steel car all trimmed in gray-green and dusty red. They named it the "Oliver Millet" and you can read the name on the side of the car in big gold letters.

This was the most sensible gesture I have ever seen by a big corporation. I really enjoy riding this car more.

I think most of the Monterey-San Francisco people commute by air these days. You flip over the hills in 40 minutes. But the air travelers never see the apricot trees loaded with fruit. And the pickers on the ladders in the morning.

Nor can you stand on the back platform and smell the wet fields by the coast in the evening. Or have a leisurely drink and an unhurried conversation with a neighbor while the sun is letting down far out on the Pacific.

I fly the airlines and find them comfortable. But there is a price on speed. The price is the luxury of spending time.

There were no small fry on the Del Monte so I could not question them on the desirability of being engineer on the express.

The engineer has competition these days, I imagine, and must keep on his toes. A small boy can be a Space Cadet or an airplane pilot. A fish-bowl helmet with built-in walkie-talkie may outweigh the peaked and striped hat.

It may be that a three-hour jump to San Francisco may seem mighty slow to a boy who goes to Mars on a 15-minute TV show.

As a matter of fact, a train seems just a little bumpy after riding in big airplanes. Those big smooth jobs that get you up 20,000 feet and slide along so you can set a glass of water on the floor.

Still, this leaves today's children without certain knowledge.

How many kids today, do you think, know that if you put the spoon in the coffee cup, the coffee will settle down and not slop over the edge?"

We *all* knew that when I rode the old Del Monte. I hadn't thought about it for years until I saw the coffee begin to bounce this morning. Then it all came back and I was as happy as if I'd found a dime in an old pair of pants.

Third man

Gallatin's in Monterey is a magnificent restaurant in an old Spanish adobe under antique spreading oak trees. The ceilings are beamed and low and candlelit. The wine comes from a small vineyard in the Santa Cruz hills.

It is surrounded by history. Frémont lived in the house across the street during the conquest of California.

It serves martinis in generous glasses and the barbecued Carmel Valley chicken is worth a long trip.

A tall gentleman in an old-fashioned dinner jacket was playing the zither, a rarity in itself. After a while he came over and introduced himself as Mr. Franz Gottschalk, who became famous playing the theme song in *The Third Man*. It is a fame he is trying to live down.

"The music of *The Third Man* theme was Vienna café music, you understand," he said. "It had never been written down. It was a high point of the picture—a haunting melody of the true Vienna."

Mr. Gottschalk said fame burst on him the minute the song was released.

"Before that I played the zither, nothing more. As soon as the song swept Europe, I was rushed to Hollywood.

"Of 15,000 members of the Musicians' Union in Los Angeles, I was the only zither player. I was the toast of the night clubs. It was chic to have me at parties.

"Over and over again I played *The Third Man* theme. Naturally, I grew tired of it."

Mr. Gottschalk passed his zither-playing hand over his artistic brow.

"Can you imagine what it is like? The same song over and over? Tum-de-dum-dedum-de-dum . . .

"I spoke to my agent about it. 'I can play other songs,' I said. 'When I played in Vienna my repertoire was wide. Beautiful songs filled with romance and authentic as sachertorte mit schlag.'

"The agent looked alarmed. He glanced about furtively to see if I had been overheard. 'Hush,' he said. 'Don't admit it. What the customers wish to hear is *The Third Man*. You will ruin yourself.'

"The pay was good," said Mr. Gottschalk, "and I had no wish to ruin myself."

The years passed and always the same request.

125

"Do you know how long that has been?"

I said I did indeed. *The Third Man* theme hit Europe in 1950. At a Roman restaurant called Mario's, beside the Roman wall, I spent a tearful evening pressing large lira notes on a violinist who played it for me.

The violin was excellent and accompanied by a rather tinny piano.

When I ran out of lira, I plied them with dollar bills. I really liked that song. The musicians were looking rather haggard when I left. Rich but haggard.

"Multiply your evening by a thousand times," said Franz Gottschalk, "and you have the story of my life since 1950.

"I got down on my knees to night-club owners and managers of cocktail lounges. 'Let me only try something else,' I begged. 'Play *The Third Man* theme,' they said. 'People are eating it up.'

"When I was desperate, I tried variations on the tune. I hoped to disguise it and slip off into something else. But they only made me play it over again. 'Play that *Third Man* thing,' they would say when I had finished the variation."

Mr. Gottschalk thinks he is tagged with the song for life.

"But I truly do have others. I played for many years in the Vienna cafés and naturally the customers did not want to hear one song. Would you care to hear some?"

I said I would be delighted. The bartender, however, was flagging for attention. He said a gentleman at the end of the bar had a request.

Mr. Gottschalk did not wait to hear the name of the request. He simply gave me a sad look and went back to the zither. Dum-de-dum-de-dum. Dum-de-dum-dedum. . . .

Real estate

The Spanish were great real estate developers. A few hundred years ago some Spanish soldiers were walking around California when they came to the Monterey Peninsula.

"O.K.," said the captain. "Cut it up in lots and put an ad in the newspapers. We will call this town Monterey."

The soldiers did not think much of the idea.

"There is no gold in these parts, Captain," they said. "And as you know, you cannot sell front footage to the Mexico City smarties these days. Unless you got a gold mine in the front yard."

"The trouble with you," said the captain, "is you have no vision. Look what Ponce de Leon did with those underwater lots in Florida. And the malarky Coronado put out on that coyote property up in New Mexico.

"Anybody with half an eye," said the captain, "can see that somebody will put a railroad through here. Likewise a main highway. Cut her up and advertise."

Well, as it turned out when the Spanish were run out, the railroad did not come through Monterey. Neither did the main highway.

This made it an exceedingly nice place to live.

Half the population of Monterey went out and fished for sardines. The other half canned them.

Over the hill in Carmel lived the artists and writers. They could not abide the smell of sardines. Except in sardine sandwiches.

Ambitious Monterey people went about tearing down the fine old Spanish adobes. They put up nice new brick buildings. Hoping the soap manufacturers would be impressed and move in a plant.

127

Things have changed a great deal. The sardines have gone. So have the sardine canners. And about the only thing left is the real estate development.

Nobody knows what happened to the sardines. One day they were gone, that's all. A lot of learned scientists have talked about changing water conditions and such. But what I think happened is the sardines suddenly got wise.

After a good many years, the boss sardine said one day:

"Hey fellers, these people are trying to can all of us!"

Thereupon they got out. A sardine is a dumb fish. But not that dumb.

There was no main highway. But there was a road off the main highway. A great many tourists came to town. They saw that there was no railroad and no main highway and the pine trees grew down to the edge of the Pacific.

They saw all the old adobe buildings that had not been torn down. They looked at the artists. They said the artists were quaint.

The artists thereupon moved out.

Monterey tore down the nice new brick buildings and put up facsimiles of the old Spanish adobes.

Real estate sold wonderfully. Mr. Bing Crosby put up a large home out at Pebble Beach.

And in fact everything turned out just about the way the Spanish captain had predicted.

The fertile abalone

> The more we take, the more they make
> In deep sea matrimony.
> Race suicide will ne'er betide
> The fertile abalone.

Down to the old wharf last night to audition the abalone. King of the shellfish. The only seafood I know that has been enshrined in song.

I know. I know. "The waiter roars it down the hall: 'You get no bread with one fish ball.'"

However, I consider when a fish has been ground into a fish ball, it has lost its identity.

This does not happen to the abalone. He is beaten. But he remains abalone to the end.

The abalone comes in a rough red half shell. About the size of a catcher's mitt. When I was in my youth around the Monterey Peninsula, you could go out and pry them off rocks. With a tire iron.

It is harder to do this today. There are more people after abalone. And I wouldn't know where to find a tire iron, which has disappeared along with the cold patch.

If you listen to real old-timers around these arty parts, they will tell you that most of the national magazines were stoked by writers who fed on abalone. It is seagoing ambrosia—I rank it with Sydney rock oysters or lobster on Martha's Vineyard.

You slice the abalone into steaks. Then you beat them. You beat and you beat until both you and the abalone are worn out. The steaks are then about a quarter-inch thick. They are covered with a batter and fried quickly in hot oil.

An abalone connoisseur will tell you it should be done three seconds on each side. You pop it in the pan. Clap your hands —clap, clap, clap. Turn it over. Clap, clap, clap. Take it out and serve.

Some years ago there was only one restaurant on the wharf. But it was so famous that Presidents came to eat there. It was called Pop Ernst's.

129

I saw when Pop Ernst pased away, the papers did quite a story on him. They recalled his kindly ways—a thundering piece of misinformation. Pop Ernst was a bad-tempered old man who slammed plates down, crying:

"Abalone!"

If he served anything else I do not remember it. Man, could he cook abalone! He watched you while you ate it. Wore a red stocking cap and a scowl. If you said it was good, he just grunted.

It is my opinion that all good cooks have impossible tempers. I think they are entitled to it. Like artists. Even more than artists. After all, you do not eat an artist's paintings.

But a cook must turn out a masterpiece. Then he must watch you eat it. It is enough to make a man perpetually mad. I am a cook and I get mad if people salt my food before they taste it. If they put ketchup on it, I will never invite them again.

Even before Pop Ernst, the writers wrote songs about the abalone. And they say one day a famous artist sat down and painted a picture of an abalone. But the picture has disappeared. It looked good enough to eat. And somebody ate it.

For art's sake

In my youth Carmel was a rather arty community. Set among forest-green pines along a crescent of white beach and the bluest ocean in the world. We fished blue bass off the gray rocks. The water was so cold it made your teeth chatter to look at it.

The water was clear off the rocks. You could see the bass swimming around, looking at your bait. When they took the hook they did not bite, just sucked at it. Like a kid sucking a lollipop. Then you *jerked!*

The town was full of artists and writers. And the trash barrel at the village post office was filled with rejection slips.

We parked our Model T's in the middle of the main street. Downhill and propped against a pine tree so they would not run away. You parked it a little to one side so you had room to turn the crank.

The test of any car around these parts was whether it would climb the Monterey-Carmel hill in *high!*

Not many could do it. It drove the car salesmen wild.

There was no gas gauge on a Model T. You pulled the seat off and uncapped the tank underneath. Then you stuck in a kind of wooden ruler down to the bottom. The part that came out wet indicated your gasoline.

We did not bother with such things. We knew when we were low on gas because the car sputtered going up the big hill. The gas fed by gravity—that is, it simply ran downhill from the tank to the carburetor.

When you were going uphill with a little gas, the carburetor was just a little higher than your gas level. That is what made it sputter.

Then you turned around and you *backed uphill!*

We were a resourceful bunch.

My rent car goes over the hill in high easily. Also they have regraded the hill. Cut it down. It is not a fair test any more.

All the cars go over pointed frontwards. What a secure life. I have seen as many as three cars at a time backing up that hill. We thought nothing of it. It added spice to life.

If my car ran out of gas today, I don't know what I'd do. Call a cab, I guess. I have lost touch with the mechanical world under the hood.

Our car hoods opened from the side—both sides. They hooked down. But the engines were so unpredictable we seldom bothered to hook them down. Why do that when you had to look underneath at any instant?

If you had somebody riding with you, he stood on the running board. He lay forward and lifted the hood and fiddled with things inside. You could flip the needle valve on the carburetor with your fingers. It gave the gasoline kind of a helping hand.

In the driver's seat you were pretty busy. Feeding with the hand throttle and retarding the spark lever. The right combination on this was more delicate than fixing a flickering TV set.

There was also a box of coils under the dashboard. You kept the top off. Once in a while you flicked them with your finger. Nearly always it gave you a powerful shock. It was supposed to be healthy, though. Some people said it made your hair grow.

The sun is on the pines this morning. And the sea is still like blue ink. The cars whizz over the cut-down hill in high. And park on the side of the street without the help of a blocking pine tree.

I drive with a gas gauge. Unshocked by shocking coils. My hair—there you have proof. No hair oil touches the vitality that used to run tingling up the arm.

Horse sense

It fairly makes my blood boil when I think of the material sawed off on me as an innocent moppet.

I was raised on *Black Beauty*. Black Beauty was a horse. He was full of love, gratitude and a banker's sense of 6 per cent on a sound investment. I wept over his problems.

In the silent cinema, loving horses gnawed the bonds that

bound the wrists of William S. Hart. I remember they used to kiss each other good-by.

In my youth, people who failed at minor problems "did not have common, ordinary horse sense."

Consequently, I grew up with a totally false view of horses.

I went up the Carmel Valley to ride one of these animals. It is very social to ride horses. Also very athletic.

The wrangler threw a saddle on the horse. "This horse will go," he assured me. "But you gotta take a rope to him if he stops. Let him know who's boss."

"Who is boss?" I asked humbly. The horse looked around. I could have sworn he was sneering. He had large teeth.

I must say that most wranglers give this advice. Beat the beast? I would no more lay a whip on these animals than I would enter a cage full of tigers. Matter of fact, I usually carry a pocketful of sugar, hoping to bribe them.

"Just ride him up the trail and let him go," said the wrangler. "He knows the way."

My horse walked off briskly like a bank messenger in sight of the vice-president. As soon as he got behind the barn, he slowed down to a shamble. By the time he got up in the shade of the oak trees, he stopped dead.

"Sugar?" I said, eagerly pushing a lump under his nose.

The horse gave me a bored smile over his shoulder. He kicked at a fly and humped his back slightly.

A pair of small children came by at a canter. My horse gave their horses a how-do-you-do. "Just stopped for a Coke," he said.

I nudged him gently with one heel.

"Nice horsie," I said, "you want to follow the other horsies? Up the hill?"

He shook his head till the bit rattled. He pawed the ground.

133

I turned him around. Immediately he threw off his worn-out attitude. He headed for the stable as if he were in the Derby.

"You gotta let him know who's boss," said the wrangler.

"I did," I said, "but he wanted to make a union case of it."

It's a menace

Mr. Hank Ketcham has moved into the Carmel Valley and is living the rich life of a rancher. The other night he came by to show me the rich bruises he got from being thrown from a quarter horse.

Mr. Ketcham keeps a quarter horse to shag cows around.

This wealthy operation is extremely simple. All you have to be able to do is draw *Dennis the Menace*.

Mr. Ketcham draws this comic panel. The idea of work seems to set Mr. Ketcham's blood aboil. He draws *Dennis* for hundreds of newspapers. Then he puts it into books and on napkins and glasses and all sorts of money-producing outlets. He is a regular dynamo of energy.

With this income, Mr. Ketcham buys horses and hay and cows to shag around the pasture and rich ointment for his bruises. It is a fine life.

It is a terrible thing to face but the idea of work affects me just the opposite.

When I think of work, I get unpleasant reactions. I sometimes feel quite ill and have to take my temperature. A man can be on the brink of the grave and have a normal temperature.

The idea of work is a bad idea. I have been thinking seriously of giving it up. I think I will go and live with the energetic Mr. Ketcham. I will rub liniment on his bruises and

134

speak sharply to his quarter horse. If the horse does not stop bruising him, I will not let him have his weekly quarter.

Mr. Ketcham is a smart man. He has a son named Dennis. When Dennis was three years old, Mr. Ketcham drew pictures of him. He sold these pictures. Naturally, Dennis grew, being a normal child.

Mr. Ketcham paid no attention. He went right on drawing Dennis the way he first sold him.

I must say I admire this type of genius. When my own child was six, I wrote little pieces about her for the paper. People read these pieces and said: "That's a bright child and says many clever things to her father."

By and by this child got to be seven. She was still bright and fairly chatty, though I was forced to edit her copy.

Yesterday she became twelve years old. Her garments have become intimate and her conversation is loaded with old jokes. She telegraphs the punch line and steps on the crusher. I do not think I could trade her for a secondhand quarter horse. I never saw a bright prospect get less commercial.

While Dennis, that small golden boy, remains bright as a new penny.

Life of the rich

Over in Pebble Beach I found Mr. Jimmy Hatlo, another cartoon gentleman. Mr. Hatlo lives in an elegant 14-room scatter where he can lean out and throw his dishwater on the rich golfers.

Of course, Mr. Hatlo does not do this. For it would cause a good deal of talk. But he could if he wanted to.

He can lean out another window and see Mr. Bing Crosby's

wash hanging on the line. Or run across the street and borrow a cup of sugar from a sugar king.

"I am hard at work," said Mr. Hatlo. He introduced me to Mr. Bob Dunn who had come all the way from New York City to work with Mr. Hatlo.

They said they were working like mad. On things like *They'll Do It Every Time* and the *Little Iodine* strip and so on.

Mr. Hatlo took me up to his studio. His drawing board faced the window looking over the Pacific. He had a built-in tracing table with a light underneath.

He had stacks of books and a big fireplace with a copper hood. He had lots of pencils laid out and a built-in darkroom and a built-in bar.

He said he was hard at work.

There was a light film of dust over everything.

"I think we will get down to *hard* work Thursday," said Mr. Dunn.

I asked him when he was going back to New York.

"Friday," said Mr. Dunn happily. "You down here on a holiday?"

"Are you kidding?" I cried. "I am hard at work. I am murdering myself with toil."

Mr. Hatlo said he would be at his drawing board that instant. But he was forced to attend a meeting of the Thirsty Thursday Club. This scientific organization studies cause and effect, he said. Such as two pair versus three-of-a-kind.

Lost and found

LOST: One swimming hole, vicinity of Carmel River. Sentimental value only. No questions asked. No questions answered.

Somewhere across the road, beyond the yellow fields and beyond the willows, at the foot of the dark olive coastal hills is the old swimming hole.

I seem to have mislaid it. They have been straightening the road around here since I was a boy. Straightening it and paving it and lining the sides with barbwire.

On the warm spring days we went down the path to the little shingle beach by a steep cliff of gray rock. The water was about 15 feet deep and in the shallows the crayfish came over and investigated your toes.

Our swimming was done without bathing suits or permission to leave school—symbol of our independence against authority.

I have looked high and low along the river. But I am afraid I shall never find it again.

The Carmel Valley is grown up these days. And the old swimming holes are tiled by Paddock and cost up to $50,000. A river crayfish nibbling at your toes would have to pay cover charge.

It is beautiful resort country. Warm sunny days and cool nights. When Carmel a few miles away is filled with fog, the valley is filled with sun, insulated by the coastal hills.

You can tell how the weather is over in Monterey by the number of people around the swimming pools. If the weather is good, few people. But when the fogs come in, the valley fills up.

The Monterey Peninsula is a good deal like Cape Cod. It is related to San Francisco as the Cape is to Boston. It has the same summer visitors, real estate operators, artists, writers. Little theatre projects, soothsayers and analysts.

It also has the same local feuds and a touch of intellectual snobbery in certain quarters. It produces elegant and expensive cocktail parties whose guests discuss the qualities of the Porsche over the Jaguar. And red wine parties in remodeled barns along Cannery Row where guests speak wisely of art.

It has a colony far down the coast at Big Sur presided over by Henry Miller. His books are banned from import. You pick them up in paperback editions in Paris and take them through customs in your hip pocket.

The valley has a tiny village, a couple of bars and a civic light opera group.

The Peninsula also has the famous 17-mile Drive and Pebble Beach Lodge, a baronial enterprise of Mr. Sam Morse, the political and social power of the area.

Up in the valley, the old ranches, cut out of Spanish land grants, are themselves being cut up into real estate developments. Long adobe ranch-house homes are built under the oaks and along the river willows.

It has all changed and nobody swims in the river, any more. I can't even find the place, these days.

Lemurians, get lost

I was driving from San Francisco to Los Angeles the other day. And since it was fine spring weather, I went over to Oceana to see how the magnetic center of the world is getting along these days.

I suppose few people know as they drive by on Highway 101

that they are close enough to magnetism to jerk the nails out of your boots. Pull the rivets clean out of your Levis.

It is a very small community. But very powerful. It has a curious history of frustration.

Oceana lies on the seaside where the curving 101 leaves Pismo Beach and plunges into the valley at Arroyo Grande.

A good many of the early settlers came up here very mad.

Some years ago you may remember that Madame Annie Besant set up a colony of Theosophists at Ojai not far from Santa Barbara.

"I have triangulated the stars and one thing and another," said Annie, "and I find this is the magnetic center of the earth."

She said this made it prime country to operate as a new spiritual leader.

I do not recall what started the fireworks. But spiritual leading is a fatiguing and irritating business, I imagine. And a few parties took off in a huff from Ojai. They set up shop near Oceana and named their community Halcyon. They issued a statement:

"This is the true magnetic center of the world," they said.

They said Annie had better get out her slide rule and look to her logarithms. Ojai, they said, didn't have enough magnetics to snatch the pins out of a set of Gandhi shorts.

Colonies like this attract some odd persons. And when I visited it some years ago I recall a gentleman who preached that milk is poison. And another who insisted on living on nothing but walnuts.

There was also a story that golden men from the Lost Continent of Lemur walked the dunes at night. And a good many ladies strolled the dunes. For a golden man is quite a catch. Certainly better than no man at all.

For all its magnetism, I do not remember that the colony ever got off the ground. While Annie Besant's group was going strong at Ojai.

There is a hexagonal temple. And you can see the great three-story gingerbread house, with empty gaping windows and steeple, where the local headman held forth. But no great leader rose to speak the great wisdom to the empty people.

The Southern Pacific sent the community into its commercial phase. One day engineers appeared and began surveying for a huge midway water and engine change station.

Overnight the citizens became real estate tycoons.

"How much you want for that corner lot?" one would say.

"I wouldn't take less than $50,000."

"Sold."

The first gentleman would then give the second gentleman his marker. For there was little money rolling about. Nevertheless, a man with a marker for 50 grand feels fairly well-to-do. And it made great changes.

The daughter of the local storekeeper broke her engagement to the delivery boy. For a lady with large sugar cannot be too careful who she marries.

A great new social structure sprang up. Ladies whose husbands held markers for a half million did not take tea with ladies who could only show tabs for a poor $100,000.

Wells were dug to water the railroad and citizens began pricing boat trips to Europe.

Then the bubble busted. For the wells came in salt. And salt water is no good for the inside of an engine. The midway stop for Southern Pacific moved up a few miles to San Luis Obispo. And the storekeeper's daughter re-engaged herself to the delivery boy.

Last of the bad men

"Boys," said Al Jennings, "they's a lot worse thieves outa the penitentiary than they is in. An' that's the record."

Mr. Al Jennings is the last of the Oklahoma train robbers. He is spry as a fiddler in his middle nineties and lives just outside Los Angeles.

I'd heard that he buried some of his loot in Texas and asked him if this were true.

"Never buried a dime," said Mr. Jennings. "Some of it I give away. But most of it was stole from me by crooked lawyers and politicians.

"Come up to Hollywood and put my money in Beesemeyer's bank. Had a couple of bars of gold. Villa's stuff. Come downtown later and they was women weepin' an' a-hollerin' outside. 'The bank's been robbed,' they says. 'Yes,' I says, 'robbed from the inside.' An' that's a fact, boys. That's history.

"I'm a killer, boys," said Mr. Jennings. "I guess you know that. Now that's the truth. Only five feet four in my boots, but a killer.

"Now killin' a man to me don't mean a gol durn thing. That was trained into me by the greatest gun fighter ever lived. Jim Stanton. That wasn't his real name, boys. His name was Hatfield. One of them West Virginia feud fellers.

"Good gosh a-mighty. If I was to tell you the things I seen. I'm a Democrat but they're just as big a bunch of thieves as the Republicans. That's all in the record, boys. I know these things. Teddy Roosevelt, himself, pardoned me.

"Why, boys, you talk of Texas. I got two chunks of lead in me right now from that fight over at the Spike S ranch. A 30-30 hit me in the laig here.

141

"Boys, Bill Irwin went over there and counted the bullet holes in that little box house. Over 400 shots filed through that place—broke all the dishes an' ever' gol durn thing an' us in there."

"Who was shooting at you, Al?"

"Bud Ledbetter an' his marshals. We whipped the whole durn bunch an' got away! Now, that's history, boys. It's all in the records.

"Frank was all shot up—that was my brother. He was a fine musician. All of us boys was trained musicians before I became an outlaw. I played the tuba. Now let me tell you about that before I fergit it.

"That's how I got outa the Ohio Penitentiary. Played a tuba solo for the warden. Now that's the truth, boys."

Mr. Jennings went in the house and came back with a big, frontier model .45 with the sights and trigger filed off.

"Now here's one of the guns I used." Mr. Jennings flipped it up from the hip. I could see the brass cartridges twinkling in the sun and said so.

"Well, I'll jist unload it," said Al. "I allus carry five in the cylinder and a empty under the hammer." He flipped the gun again and fanned the hammer with his thumb. I noticed there were only four shells emptied on the ground.

Mr. Jennings was throwing down on a lady who was bending over in the vegetable garden. I mentioned the missing shell.

"I guess I forgot one," said Al casually opening the gun and extracting the bullet.

"That's Maud, my wife," he explained. "She was a great friend of Jesse James.

"Now it was in the pen I saw Bill Porter again. O. Henry was the name he wrote under. Met him first down in Honduras. Asked him to rob a bank with me but he wouldn't. I put $2000 in his pocket, anyway."

"Al," I said, "didn't you bury one little ol' bag of loot down in Texas? I could dig it up for you."

"Not a cent," said Mr. Jennings regretfully. "That was jist a story I told the guard to get him to smuggle in a saw. That pen bored me, I wanted to git out. 'Slip me the briers an' I'll dig up the loot,' I says. An' he done it.

"They sent me up for life plus five years for shootin' Bud Ledbetter. But, boys, they had no warrant for us. We was entitled to defend ourselves. I ain't against a marshal killin' you, an' then readin' the warrant after you're dead. But they didn't even know who we was. They was after me for stealin' a saddle at a time. An' that's history, boys. I swear to Heaven!"

Rich and happy

I am concerned about the economy of the country, but I do not waste time with Dow-Jones averages or watch ticker tape. I watch rich people. If they are happy, I feel the country is on a sound footing. So I went to Palm Springs for a look.

All along the highway were signs inviting me to buy dates. They raise dates around here and are so busy unloading them they put them in milk shakes.

A few years ago the country was mainly desert with a few Indians. Then it became fashionable to go to the desert. People came and built great resorts. The Government sent the Indians to school and some of them became lawyers.

One day an Indian lawyer came home and looked in his lawbooks.

143

"Hey, Chief," he said. "The way I read this statute, this desert belongs to us. All these rich people are nothing but nesters and we can get the law on them."

The courts, as I recall, agreed with them. The Indians prepared to move into the Mirador and Biltmore and the Racquet Club and other multimillion-dollar resorts. But as you know, a court decision does not always mean you have to give back the marbles. Not until you ask other courts if the first court was right.

I do not know what happened. But everybody seemed happy enough, so I assume the invasion was staved off.

I checked in at La Paz Guest Ranch, a pretty acreage of tiled cottages on the edge of town. There is a fine swimming pool, tennis courts and stables. A nine-hole golf course was in the making. It was the liveliest place in Palm Springs.

Well, there is nothing that I admire more than justice. And I am happy to knock this idle rumor of the idle rich. The rich around Palm Springs are terribly industrious, playing tennis and riding horses and all sorts of strenuous activities. They seemed quite happy.

Toward evening they all went to their rooms, possibly to clip coupons. (You should always clip your coupons and never bite them, you know that.)

Later they appeared in the cocktail lounge. And many visitors came in and joined the party. I assume everybody was rich because that is the way I like to think of Palm Springs. Rich and happy.

Mr. Bob Hope came over for dinner and an aperitif. And it is a known fact that Mr. Hope has picked up a biscuit or two from moving pictures and TV.

Miss Gussie Moran came in with Mr. Eddie Hand. Mr. Hand, I hear, has been frugal and salted something away. Miss

Gussie Moran is the tennis lady who first displayed frilled panties in the game. I consider this as important as the little scrub who ran with the ball at Rugby, thus starting American football and college careers for steelworkers.

"Baby, it's cold outside"

In 1867 there was a tremendous ski race in the Sierra. Mr. Robert Oliver of Sawpit was adjudged the greatest skier in California.

Afterward Mr. Creed Haymond was chosen president of the club at a meeting at Logan's saloon. The correspondent reported that he "made a little boy's speech through which ran his usual vein of humor. . . ."

This was followed by "cheers for Haymond, cheers for the champion of the belt and last, but by no means least, were the cheers given for the winner of the leather medal. . . .

"Cheers for the ladies were followed by songs among which were the following: 'No Irish Need Apply' and 'Beautiful Star.'

"The band struck up a march. The meeting formed itself into a procession and marched to the Masonic Hall where a ball closed the festive scenes of the racing season."

The other day I drove up to the snow country for the opening of the season.

Baby, it was cold outside! So I did not go outside. I watched the skiers through the big picture windows beside the fire in the lodge.

This is my idea of how to spend the ski season.

A skier's idea is entirely different.

A skier comes down beside the fire in his ski pants. He sits down and puts on his ski boots. It is a fearful process. They lace front and back and have wonderful steel tips in case you should want to kick somebody.

I think the skier is all bound in around the waist. When he gets up from tying his ski boots, he is all out of breath.

He goes out in the cold, cold snow, puts on his skis and rides a chair lift up to the top of the mountain.

He then slides down. That is all there is to it.

Sometimes on the way down he breaks a leg. Then the ski patrol brings him down on a toboggan. He spends the rest of the season on the front porch. With people writing funny remarks on his white plaster cast.

This is considered great sport.

I cannot think of anything similar. Except a soldier I talked to in Tripler Hospital in Honolulu.

"Tough luck," I said. "Korea?"

"Great luck," he said. "I broke it falling off a bar stool in the Kona Club. Just before they were going to ship me to Korea."

Maybe it is like that with skiing. The next run you might have broken your neck. There is no place to write on a broken neck.

The big meet in 1867 was the first ski meet in America. (That is what they tell me here anyway.)

Mr. Creed Haymond was the big man. Mr. Haymond was a high-priced lawyer for the Southern Pacific. In early days he carried the mail on skis between La Porte and Gibsonville and Poker Flat.

California skiers claim this is the hundredth anniversary of skiing in California. They date it back a little before "Snowshoe" Thompson who carried the winter mail at $1 a letter between Virginia City and Hangtown.

146

Ski resorts consist largely of big fireplaces, White Stag sweaters, much talk about ski wax, hot buttered rum, Austrian accents and accordion playing in the evenings.

The correspondent of 1867 reported that the famous "Snowshoe" Thompson attended the big race at La Porte.

"Thompson had heard of the snowshoe races and to satisfy his curiosity, he attended those at La Porte. He veni, vided, but did not vici a bit. In fact, when he saw some of the runners make a trip, he said he did not want any in his."

"Snowshoe" and I have a good deal in common, I think.

Olympic boy

I asked Mr. Alexander Cushing how he got the 1960 Winter Olympics for Squaw Valley.

He said he read in the papers one day that competitive Reno, 30 miles away, had applied for the Olympics.

"So I just called up our press agent and said, 'Let's apply, too.'"

"You mean all you had to do was ask? Then they gave you the Games?"

"Not exactly," said Mr. Cushing. "We had to go back East and make a presentation. A lot of local people began writing me letters saying what a fine thing it was. So I thought we better give them a little run for the money.

"Speaking of money," said Mr. Cushing, "we didn't have a dime to lay on the table. But Governor Knight gave us a strong statement that he would ask for a million dollars from the Legislature.

"We made a talk to the committee in New York and all of a sudden, there we were. Picked as the United States offering for the Olympics."

147

"Does the committee help you after that?"

"No. All they do is tell you, 'You're the choice. Now you go ahead.' I didn't have any idea what to do then. So I went over to Europe and looked around. I'd never seen any skiing in Europe and it was a good excuse."

Around Europe everybody told Cushing that the fix was for Innsbruck in 1960. In fact, they felt a little sorry for the country boy.

"Then I ran into George Weller, the foreign correspondent. He said, 'What are you doing over here?'

"I said, 'I'm trying to get the Olympic Games for the United States.'

"He said, 'Where's the rest of your party? Where's your committees?'

"I said, 'I'm all alone. Just me.' That got him interested."

The outcome was that Weller got a little time off from his job. He began spreading the word.

"There are 72 members of the Olympic committee who decide where the games go and they're spread out in 40 countries all over the world. We decided to concentrate on South America.

"I guess it was flattering. Or maybe it sounded cool," said Cushing. "Our argument was the winter Olympics had been held in Europe for 28 years. But the real key to the thing was that the committee meeting was in Paris.

"It isn't a question of voting. It's a question of voting in person. All the South Americans were red-hot for an excuse to go to Paris. They had the biggest meeting they ever had."

Cushing said all of the South Americans went to Paris. "And all but 12 voted for us."

Cushing went around to see Avery Brundage, the American Olympic wheel. "I'm from Squaw Valley," said Cushing.

"What's that?" said Brundage. Then he gave Cushing some advice.

"If you can impress the committee that you exist this year, you'll have done a good job. You might get something in 1964. This year, no chance."

"But a lot of Europeans said they might give us a vote on the first ballot. Just to encourage us. Help the country boys along, you might say."

The European contingent suddenly woke up to find the poor country boys had 70 per cent of the votes. The Europeans made a desperate effort to recover. But the avalanche was on.

Ski pants

The sun came out warm on the snow-pack. And a couple of off-course robins sat around blinking their eyes and wondering whatever happened to April, eh?

All the squaws at Squaw Valley put on their tight, tight ski pants. And their tight, tight ski sweaters. And sat around parlaying the million-dollar view into two million.

I do not understand why skiing must be done in a costume that is pasted on. But I am a philosophical bloke. If a Squaw Valley squaw gets between you and the scenery, what do you want? Eggs in your beer?

There is no snowman more abominable than the snowman who avoids the snow. To my mind, snow is for snowballs. A sport I gave up in my salad days.

Snow, I have discovered, is not just white stuff that falls out of the sky. It is ice. It is powder. It is corn.

I am practically illiterate at this sort of conversation.

"How did you come down?" said a skier professionally.

"Well," I said miserably. "I just sort of waded."

"Ice?" he said knowingly.

"No, thank you," I said. "I just take it straight. With a little soda on the side."

"What kind of wax are you using?"

"For heaven's sake, man," I said, "are you mad? I can hardly stand up as it is."

I met another skier. He said there was nothing to it. He had skied two days.

"Just rented a pair of skis and started down."

"What happened?"

"I got picked up by the ski patrol right away," he said proudly.

"What for?"

"I went between two skiers. You aren't supposed to go between two skiers. You know what I told them? I said, 'Look, where do you think I could go? These things got no brakes on them!'"

NEVADA

When the sun settles below the jagged mountains, Reno comes to life.

The Truckee River cuts through the town. Not an oily river filled with factory waste that you find on the Atlantic seaboard. It is a rushing little trout stream, gurgling over a gravel bed and curving around aspen banks.

The moonlight spills a flood of silver on the water. And on opposite sides rise the brightly lighted Mapes and Riverside Hotels.

Neons blaze from the Truckee along Virginia Street to Harold's Club. A lighted sign across the street declares:

The Biggest Little City in the World

100,000 slot machines

Somebody in Reno estimated for me that there are more than 100,000 slot machines in Nevada. The last frontier for slot machines.

All up and down the streets, the slot machines set up a steady chatter. Pull, whir, clatter, crash. Night and day. For Nevada's legal gambling houses are open 24 hours.

"A slot machine has no dealer and needs only a little servicing," said Bernie Einstoss, the Reno gambler. "We can pay back 92 per cent and make money on the grind.

"Give me the slot-machine concession in Grand Central Station and I'll pay the national debt."

There is a fascination in the whirling wheels with the cherries, oranges and elusive bars of the jackpot.

Professor B. F. Skinner of Harvard University decided to find out what made people pull levers hour after hour. The first thing he did was get some slot machines and some chimpanzees. Because as all psychologists know, people are like chimpanzees and vice versa.

First they loaded the slot machines with bananas. When the chimp pulled the lever he got a banana.

Then they rigged the machine so he had to get the combination to get the banana.

Then they fixed the machine so he just got something that *looked* like a banana.

152

The chimps did not give a hoot. They were hooked. They went right on playing. Just like the ladies who sit all day in front of the machines at all the clubs.

They fixed the machines so that the chimp only got a poker chip payoff. The chimp went right on playing anyway.

A man who runs the machines at one of the big clubs said he thought it was a terrible thing to teach a chimp.

"Next thing you know, they will teach those monkeys how to spoon a machine."

Spooning a machine is tripping it so it pays off illegally. You run a device down the slot so that you don't have to drop in nickels or quarters or silver dollars.

"If some of these people spent as much time as they do making things to beat the house, they could make a rocket that would reach the moon," he said.

Real slot-machine addicts play two or three machines at a time. The management is helpful. They give the person a stool to sit on.

The idea seems to be to hit the jackpot. Many Nevada machines are set up to hit more than the usual number of jackpots. But they are also set to give smaller numbers of small payoffs.

The players don't seem to care. As fast as it comes out they put it back in. They don't care what comes out. Silver dollars or bananas. I asked the gambler why he didn't just fill the machines with bananas. He said he didn't want to encourage a lot of educated chimps to come around and play the machines.

"Get a place full of monkeys playing the slots, it might give the house a funny reputation."

"You can't take it with you"

I stepped through the neon glitter and glass front of Harold's Club and put 50 cents in the slot machine.

It was like stepping on a burglar alarm. The machine coughed fiercely and began spitting half dollars at me. The top lighted up. Bells rang. Men shouted and women fainted.

The manager came over and switched off the judas.

"Do you realize what you have done?" he asked.

"I don't talk without my mouthpiece," I said nervously. "However, I didn't mean to break the mechanism, Your Honor. I merely pulled this little old lever and—"

"You have won the $75 super-duper jackpot. Oh, happy day for Harold's Club! Here." He began stuffing my pockets with bills.

"For me?"

"But certainly. We *love* to give money away. Confidentially," said the manager, "we would like to give you more. But that is what your wager won. Perhaps the next time you will do better."

It seems odd that with such philanthropy the club changed owners once for something around $12,000,000.

It opened in 1935. Since 1940 it has never closed. Open 24 hours a day.

Escalators lift the guests gently through seven floors of chance. It has four or five bars, a pigeonhole parking lot and a motel for the weary.

When gambling was a gentleman's pursuit in Nevada, Harold's electrified the business by putting in girl dealers.

Gambling here is on a department-store basis.

154

"You mean all these gaming devices are just ways of giving the customer money?" I asked.

"We do our best," said the manager. "We provide you with 750 slot machines, some paying off over $100 on the jackpot. We offer 13 dice tables, 10 roulette layouts and 40 odd black-jack deals.

"Not to mention panguingui, horserace keno, chuck-a-luck, bingo, lottery, poker and many other games of fun and frolic."

"The owner is a philanthropist?"

"What is money?" said the manager. "You can't take it with you."

At short intervals slot machines lit up and rang in the rooms. And officials rushed over with handfuls of green bills.

"Business is good," said the manager. "And now perhaps you wish to wager some more of your glue?"

"I hate to take your money."

"Why that is what we are here for," he said cheerfully. "The owner does not wish to keep his money. For after all, it is merely dross you might say and you can't take it with you."

And now, after several hours at the slot machine, I think he never said anything truer.

Sugar daddy

Mr. George Sanchez who owns most of the sugar in Cuba is in town. A sure sign that Mr. Joe E. Lewis, the comedian, is not far behind.

Besides Cuban sugar, Mr. Sanchez is loaded with umpty thousand Cuban cattle, a railroad and such million-dollar equipment at Camaguey.

This is very fortunate. For Mr. Sanchez has an expensive hobby. Mr. Sanchez is a night-club buff.

Fire buffs follow fires, with a ticker rapping out the alarms in the bedroom. Police buffs follow police calls.

Mr. Sanchez follows night-club performers. From town to town. Engagement to engagement. This is his Joe E. Lewis period. The comedian is due shortly at Mert Wertheimer's gaming casino at the Riverside. And Mr. Sanchez will be waiting happily. Center table, ringside.

For a long time Mr. Sanchez followed Helen Morgan. He built his Miami home in the heart of the night-club district, with a bar that is an exact replica of the taproom in New York's swank "21."

While sitting about waiting for the evening show to go on, Mr. Sanchez charters a bus and takes the entire chorus line on caviar-and-champagne picnics.

Except for the late hours, it looks like a delightful life.

Mr. Lou Wertheimer filled me in on all of this while I was sitting by the Riverside pool one day. He said Mr. Sanchez has been sugaring shows since 1908 and is as fresh as the day he first gandered a Ziegfeld Follies.

Mr. Sanchez could not come to lunch.

"I must go to the dentist today," he told Mr. Wertheimer.

Mr. Wertheimer was shocked.

"This is a first-class joint," he said. "What do you mean go to the dentist? Give your teeth to a bellboy and we'll send them over."

Mr. Sanchez is a constant source of amazement to the management.

"Yesterday he bought a big refrigerator and sent it up to his room," said Lou Wertheimer. "Why? He likes melons. He said the hotel refrigerator in his room was not big enough to hold melons.

"Nighttimes he sees the shows. Daytimes he goes down and feeds the fish."

"Feeds the fish?" I said.

"Feeds the fish. He goes outside by the Truckee River and feeds the trout. Carries a big loaf of bread in his hand. When he is up here in the fall, he feeds the ducks."

Mr. Sanchez, he said, carries a notebook with details of which shores of the river he has fed each day.

"He plays the ducks like a system," said Mr. Wertheimer, the gambling man.

Orange blossom time

Nevada's six-week divorce law is not as profitable to "The Biggest Little City" as the orange blossom trail.

Five times as many people get married in Reno as get divorced. Both rebounds and new customers.

Marriage is so popular in the Washoe Valley that hotels offer a package price splicing: Minister, flowers, wedding supper and breakfast, and the bridal suite.

"How much?" I asked Mr. Walter Ramage, the Mapes innkeeper.

"For how long?" he asked.

"How long a marriage?" I said. "What kind of a deal is that?"

"Oh," said Mr. Ramage, "I thought you were getting married. I meant how long are you going to be here. I could give you an attractive rate."

"Speak impersonally, please," I said. "This is for publication."

"In that case," said he, "we offer a lovely ceremony for two with witnesses. A high-type preacher, flowers, champagne supper and the bridal suite for fifty dollars. You could lose that much on the tables in half an hour."

The sagebrush desert around Reno blossoms with guest ranches for ladies sitting out their six weeks' divorce residence. The guest ranches offer moonlight horseback rides, singing cowboys and station-wagon service to and from the gambling casino of the town.

Statistically, it looks like a good thing. There are two men for every woman in Nevada. But as a lady declared to me:

"It depends on which two you are issued. My two are pretty bad."

The home-talent boys have been pretty well picked over by the talent of other years. And what is left are desert rat prospectors or confirmed bachelors.

Reno's 20,000 marriages a year make the Justice of Peace election more exciting than the Governor's. Marriages pay off better than slot machines.

The judges hardly hear one "I do" before they begin the next "Dearly Beloved."

Florists profit by love in bloom. So do restaurants and hotels and champagne salesmen.

And the divorce business booms right along. Just as it has since Mary Pickford brought it to national attention in 1916 when she did her six weeks in Minden.

One for the road

At an early hour I left Reno with all pockets sagging with silver dollars. Reno issues all change in silver dollars. My change from newspapers sagged my side pockets. Change from the garage sagged others. My pistol pocket was still clanking from breakfast.

Mr. Robert de Roos, the writing gentleman, was traveling with me. And Walter Ramage at the Mapes Hotel had one of their traveling lunches packed for us. The box carries the title: *One for the Road.*

It was filled with fried chicken and tomato slices and hard-boiled eggs and orange slices and cake and pickles and so on.

One hour out of Reno we took a peek in the box. And immediately sat down under a tree beside the Truckee and had a picnic. There is nothing better than eating a picnic lunch right after breakfast. It is sort of cheating. Which makes it more fun.

Fall is a wonderful time of year to cross the desert. Highway 40 runs straight and wide, 532 miles to Salt Lake City. The air is brisk and carries a flavor of the gray-green sage.

The jump to the sink, where the Humboldt River spreads into the alkali flats, was pure murder to the wagon trains of the early days.

"Nearly all the weak stock gave out here and died," my great-grandfather wrote in 1850.

He counted more than 3000 dead oxen, horses and mules as he crossed the desert.

Now you clip off the route to Salt Lake City in one day.

Still, by habit, nearly every car carries a desert water bag. The evaporating flax bag that cools itself. I crossed here in a Model-T Ford in 1928. It took me three days on unpaved washboard desert road.

We did all driving at night. Because cars heated up so badly in the daytime.

Practically every road sign was shot out so you could not read it. Hardly any self-respecting man would pass a road sign without taking a shot at it. It was understood that road signs were put up by the State as targets.

You were supposed to know your way anyway. Since many side roads ran off to mines in the desert, you sort of navigated by guess and the deepest ruts.

When I got to Salt Lake City, the whole back of my car fell off in the road. Every bolt had been shaken out of it.

The desert was quite an adventure. You sat in a gas station before crossing and interviewed incoming cars on the state of affairs out there. Then you checked your tire patches and set out.

The road today is filled with traffic. And there are plenty of towns where you can get gas and water and a sandwich and television.

Nobody shoots up the road signs any more. For we have all become civilized.

You do not wander off on desert roads. Because Highway 40 is plainly marked at every crossroads.

Nor do we cross at night. Because our cars no longer heat up in the heat of summer.

Nor did I have to wait and interview an arrogant and dusty arriving traveler. And stand humbly listening to his advice on crossing.

In fact, the pioneer days are pretty near over, I would say.

About the only thing left is the desert water bag. Which we cling to as man clings to his outmoded appendix.

Out where the West begins

No town in America glitters like Las Vegas.

"Like one of the old Tex Guinan shows," said Ben Goffstein

160

at the multimillion-dollar Riviera. "With rhinestone G-strings and plenty of electricity."

The Strip is so crowded with plush hotels and elegant gambling houses that Johnny-come-latelys are crowding onto Boulder Highway. Modest motels are remodeling into Class A hotels.

During the day, Las Vegas visitors relax in air-cooled hotel rooms. Or sit beside the deep blue swimming pools and the tanned ladies who surround them.

From the dark, cool casinos comes the soothing clatter of dice on the green felt tables.

They say 2,000,000 people visit Las Vegas every year. The gambling tables run 24 hours a day.

Lady Luck never made herself so available.

Lest you forget, the sugar cubes are wrapped with red-and-white dice markings.

Lest you lose your way, all roads lead to the gambling room.

The action is so brisk that Las Vegas has little need of shills, paid players working with house money. You need shills on a cold table. Gamblers are as shy about sitting at an empty table as the first couple on a dance floor.

Shilling is a respectable business in Nevada. And many a divorcee sits out her six weeks playing house money at $5 a day.

You spot the shills by their small bets on slow tables. They carry no purses, for managers see no need to tempt the light-fingered.

A man shill reaching into his shirt pocket for a cigarette brushes his palms together first. This eliminates palming tricks.

At night the town blooms with light like some great juke box set down in the desert.

Green lights pour color onto the sunburnt straggling palm trees. The swimming pools glow with underwater blue spots.

The tanned ladies leave the swimming pools and reappear in strapless evening gowns. The gentlemen come back in brilliant sports shirts and cashmere jackets. The $100 bills flutter onto the green felt. Red-and-white dice spin across the stacks of gleaming silver dollars.

Music rolls out of the packed dining rooms. The spotlights focus on the biggest names in show business. The big convertibles roar up and down the Strip, bright and brilliant in an endless carnival.

High above the desert shine the lucky stars.

Boomtown, U.S.A.

From a prospectors' haven of a few thousand hopeful souls, Las Vegas has mushroomed in the desert to over 40,000 boomtown citizens.

What it is today began with a heavy influx of eastern gambling money. Benjamin "Bugsy" Siegel led the big money when he built the $7,000,000 Flamingo.

Mr. Siegel had high ideals. He insisted on evening dress and once offered to punch the nose of a guest who showed up in a sport jacket.

"Are you trying to louse up a class joint?" demanded Mr. Siegel menacingly.

Mr. Siegel ran afoul of competitive action a year later and was marred permanently by a handful of carbine bullets. The present management is more agreeable.

They only demand that you wear clothing with enough pockets to carry cash.

Mr. Siegel had in mind something patterned after the plush gambling operations in Florida.

162

He had little construction experience. But he dealt only in the best. The Flamingo is underlaid with miles of black-market copper plumbing.

"Benny never dealt with squares," a gambler told me. "He had no faith, you might say, in a guy on the legit. If Benny needed a pound of carpenter nails, he would not go to a hardware store.

"He would call up a guy in the rackets. Consequently, he paid a good many times the price. On the other hand, the guy who sold knew Benny. You could depend on it they were *good* carpenter nails. Or else!"

The gratifying boom has changed the gambling gentlemen into Chamber of Commerce-minded citizens. Models of deportment.

Meetings are held to discuss the future of Las Vegas. They are as soberly interested in sewer bonds as any thriving small town that has just captured an industrial plant.

Howdy Podner, say the big bill boards on the incoming highways.

The visiting tourist is greeted with Western hospitality, a good deal of which has undertones of Saturday matinees and Brooklyn crap games.

The gambling men urge each other on to higher endeavor.

"I ain't got no time for dat kind of blankety-blank joik," said a Strip operator at a recent meeting.

"What kind of language is dat?" said a companion. "Watch it."

"What's wrong wit' my language?" said the operator.

"It's a double negatif, dat's what," said the other triumphantly.

The first man to get the Chamber of Commerce feeling was the operator of the Arizona Club, a combination house of gambling and ladies. It flourished as a prospectors' haven when the town was a whistle stop.

When the Last Frontier was building, the owners looked through old Las Vegas for a flavor of the Old West. They found it in the leaded glass swinging doors and the bullet-scarred bar of the Arizona Club.

They bought the works on the spot.

The proprietor of the Arizona Club delivered the swinging doors but pleaded for a few days time on the bar. It was quite a bar. With knife scars and the patina of years of bourbon whiskey polished by denim sleeves.

He delivered the bar several days later. The buyers nearly fainted. The bullet holes were plugged. It had been varnished.

"I wanted you boys to have the best," said the Arizona Club man proudly. "I reckon this town is going to boom."

ARIZONA

Arizona is called the Valentine State. Because it was admitted to the Union on Valentine's Day in 1912. There was a woman in the first Legislature. Women were highly thought of in the Old West, ma'am. Still are in the new West. But there are more of 'em these days.

The state has more National Monuments than any other state. The best known is privately owned. The meteor crater near Flagstaff is owned by an Eastern mining company.

This meteor fell on Arizona and, while they don't know how to dig it out, they have determined that it is mostly iron. The Indians have a legend about the meteor. But they figured out a long time ago there was no point in mining iron when you can sell turquoise jewelry to tourists at these prices.

Cacti and camels

The country is largely cactus and it is against the law to pick cactus. Though there is no law that the cactus can't pick you.

The rented horses in Arizona know all about this cactus. They have it figured so fine they can scrape a tourist along 30 miles of it without getting a single thorn in their own hides.

There is a type of cactus called cholla cactus that looks like large burs. If you touch it, they will be pulling spines out of your great-grandchildren.

The main cactus—the kind you see in pictures and get rubbed against by horses—is the saguaro cactus. It stands 10 feet tall and has arms. It gets to be 400 years old and swells with water when there is water and shrinks when there isn't.

After 400 years it gets tired of swelling and shrinking and dies. The cactus wren is the state bird. Being state bird is quite a job, I imagine. The cactus wrens build nests in the dead saguaro.

The reason they do this is so the Indians can cut out the nests and make baskets and sell to the tourists. The tourists use them for sewing baskets and the cactus wren has to work hard to supply the demand.

Back around 1856, a Navy officer named Ed Beale persuaded Jefferson Davis to buy camels to use for transport in the desert. If there had been a drop of water in Arizona the admirals never would have stood for this. But there was hardly enough water to swell the saguaro.

The camels hauled troop supplies until 1860. The supplies were mainly bullets to shoot Indians who were not satisfied to make sewing baskets out of wren nests and liked to raise hair without irrigation.

Since this was a Navy project, the reason for the end of the camel caravans is rather curious.

They were abandoned because the camel gait made Americans seasick.

The camels were just turned loose on the desert where they did the best they could.

Wild camels were still being reported as late as 1895. But I have been unable to find the man who saw the last camel.

Mr. Bobbie Burns over at the Phoenix Chamber of Commerce said he thought camels had been seen quite recently.

But he admitted they had been sighted by cowboys who had also sighted pink elephants and other curious animals. Especially around New Year's Day.

He said it was prime camel country, though. And it would be a wonderful thing if there were camels around. Especially since the main tourist resorts are located around Camelback Mountain.

He had a wonderful idea, too.

He would like to buy a camel. Not a new camel. But a used camel with quite a bit of mileage left in him. He would take this camel out and turn him loose on the desert. And tourists sighting this camel would raise a rash of newspaper stories that would make a happy day for a press agent.

So far he has been unable to convince the Chamber of Commerce. It appears that camels, even used camels, are more expensive than a Cadillac.

Water over the dam

I don't hear so much about water these days in Arizona. A few years ago you could get a terrible argument about water. And if you were arguing from the California viewpoint, you were lucky not to get hanged.

The reason for this was pretty simple. The Colorado River runs mostly through Arizona. Until it gets toward the end where it becomes the border between California and Arizona.

At this point, it gets dammed up by Boulder Dam. Los Angeles then puts a tube in it and runs the water over to Los Angeles, where they put it on orange groves and lawns in the San Fernando Valley.

You would be surprised how mad this made the people of Arizona.

"Hey!" they said. "Where you going with all our water?"

"Why," said the people of Los Angeles, "that is our water. For, as you can plainly see, it is running out the tube over this way. As to what we are going to do with it, we are going to drink it. Sometimes plain and sometimes with rifle whiskey. Or make it into lemonade with our incomparable California lemons.

"We shall also take baths with it and put it in flower pots and whatever else is good to do with water."

"But that water runs through our state," said the people of Arizona.

"Not at our end," said the people of Los Angeles. "At our end it is running right out of our faucets. So kindly be careful how you handle it in your state and don't wade in it or anything. We like our water clean and fresh."

So that Arizona would not do anything rash about this

water with Congress, they set up a lobby in Washington. To show Congress the true state of affairs and how this water belonged to Los Angeles.

The man they put in charge was Mr. John U. Terrell. Mr. Terrell having been a colleague of mine in the newsboy business, I know a lot about the situation.

He explained it all to me at the Washington Press Club one day.

"There would be no point in Arizona getting all that water," said Mr. Terrell. "Because it is all desert."

The Arizona people used to fuss a lot about this in Washington. They said by the great horned toad, Los Angeles was all desert, too. Except they had all the water.

Recently, I have not heard too much about water. The orange groves where Arizonans used to put the water have all been cut up into building lots. You know who builds on them? Californians who can't stand the watery California winter weather.

It takes a certain amount of rain to make any state go. And Arizona looks forward to its rain.

The rain comes in the winter season. Just like California. As a matter of fact, Arizona rain is the rain left over from what comes down on California. This also makes the Arizona people hopping mad, but there is not much they can do about it.

When the rainy season comes around, the Hopi Indians up north get a mouthful of rattlesnakes and go dancing around for rain. They usually get it, too.

They dance for rain so successfully that over in New Mexico the other Indians had to change the date of some of their dances. The Hopis danced a week before and flooded out the opposition.

The California tourists go up and watch the Indians dance for rain. They take their photographic equipment and shoot color pictures and say, "Boy, they'll never believe this back home."

Then the Hopis turn the rattlesnakes loose and the rattlesnakes go down in their holes and tell the rain gods: "Some of those Californians around again. Wet 'em down."

And the rain comes down. And the California tourists say, "Heavenly days, what weather. I came here for the sun." And they go back home and drink the Arizona water. And this makes Arizona madder than ever. It gets very complicated and not even Congress has been able to straighten it out.

Dog days

While the East was full of snow and the West Coast was full of rain, the people of Arizona sat under sunny skies and counted the tourist money.

The desert days run about 70 degrees and the desert nights drop to a chill 40. The sun comes out daily as if it were on the Chamber of Commerce payroll. And the blue-jeaned tourist puts on his high-heeled boots and his Navajo turquoise belt and lives it up, man, lives it up.

There was a time when Arizona was toured mainly by people with weak lungs, as my grandma used to put it. It is a terribly healthy state, and today's tourists whose lungs are O.K. get out and breathe great breaths of dry desert air.

The climate is so good I thought I should go over and see a dog I had heard about named Caesar.

Caesar is a seven-months-old Boxer. He came out here for his asthma. I imagine he is the only dog in the world who comes to Arizona for his asthma. It does him a world of good.

170

Caesar is a guest at the Canine Country Club. He is owned by a lady from Bronxville, N.Y.

"He was wheezing like a steam engine when he arrived," said the doctor in charge. "Now look at him."

I looked at Caesar and he looked at me. Caesar did some deep breathing exercises. He licked my hand, barking softly. Nary a wheeze.

"I gave him a little treatment," said the doctor. "But the climate did most of it. Dry desert air. The Phoenix sun treatment."

The doctor himself spent 30 years in the New York area. Then he came to Phoenix on account of the climate. He does not wheeze either.

The "yep" and "nope" man

One of the main industries here is the dude ranch. And I went to Wickenburg to watch the cowboys sashay around in their $40 britches.

I have concluded that it is well worth while. If I had the money I would go out and be a dude. Better, I would buy myself a dude ranch and charge dudes high prices for sitting on the empty saddles in my old corral.

Once when I was duding around one of these spreads, I used to go down and see the head dude wrangler who, naturally, was called "Tex."

Tex read Western stories by the bucketful—he had a whole pile of them stashed in his bedroom. All worn and thumbed.

He knew how a cowboy should act therefore. A cowboy should be stern and closemouthed. I rarely heard Tex mutter more than "yep" or "nope."

"Do you like this work?" I asked.

"Yep."

"Ever think about doing anything else?"

"Nope."

"Why not?"

"Good job."

Right then I could see that dude ranching was the business. You can get a "yep" and "nope" man for pretty low wages. And I doubt if they are in a union. Because I do not see how you can hold a union meeting with so little conversation.

After a few days of this I concluded Tex was a moron. I figured they were holding him there for slave labor. Paying him off probably with old Western magazines and jellybeans.

The only long speech I ever heard was:

"This hoss don't like that hoss."

Since this hoss had just kicked that hoss, I could have drawn the same conclusion. And it wouldn't have taken me 40 years on the range either. However, now it seems to me that Tex frankly was puzzled that all these dudes would pay out $50 a day just to watch one hoss kick another hoss. For that was about all that happened at this dude ranch.

People who do not go to dude ranches go to winter resorts. And the most curious around here is Arizona Main Chance Farm.

The Arizona Main Chance Farm is harder to get into than it is to get out of Alcatraz. It is a reducing farm.

It is a reducing farm run by Elizabeth Arden, the beauty lady.

The tariff is $600 a week and the reducing farm takes only 21 guests.

At $600, ladies are put into better condition—better condition to many ladies being to lose a few pounds.

Miss Arden reduces them $600 and six pounds per week. Meantime, they work like dogs from 9 to 5 every day. They fodder them up with orange juice and lettuce leaves and skim milk. And slather them with all kinds of beauty creams.

When a lady comes out she is all oiled and trim.

I called up and tried to speak to Perle Mesta and Clare Booth Luce, both going through the arduous Arden treatment. But the lady at Main Chance said there wasn't a chance.

"All inquiries must be cleared through Miss Arden in New York."

I did find out, however, that it takes 32 employees at Main Chance to hammer 21 dollies. But at $600 per you can hire an awful lot of hammering.

Though this cannot compare with dude ranching, I imagine. Where one employee says "yep" and "nope." And lets the hosses do the hammering.

10-gallon women in 5-gallon Levis

Mr. Jack Stewart out at Camelback Inn phoned me one morning.

"Can you have lunch?" he asked. "And what are you doing in town?"

I said I was here to banish care and woe. (That is the way I talk when the poetic streak is on me—when I look out toward Camelback, breathe deeply of the desert air. And then go back in and go to bed again.)

"Also," I said, "I am here to avoid the scent of printer's ink. Which, as you must know if you see newspaper movies, runs deeply in our veins. In short, I am trying to get away from it all."

"This is a curious time you have chosen," said Mr. Stewart. "For 60 newspapermen arrive in the morning."

And so here we are. Living it up around Camelback with enough reporters to put out a Sunday edition.

Nobody gives out with Western talk like: "He went thataway." Or, "I reckon the schoolmarm is a mighty pretty critter."

All they talk about is, "Do you remember when we were working the Red Carnation murder? Now I always said—"

I shoulda stood in the Press Club somewhere.

Well, this is where the West begins. I read this in the travel brochures, too.

This is where men get into 10-gallon hats and 40-gallon boots. And women get into Levis—size 10-gallon women get into size 5-gallon Levis, that is. I have often wondered how they do it.

Matter of fact, I have often wondered how they sit down. Or how they get up. These are the tightest pants you ever saw.

No lady feels she has really arrived until she has dusted down to Porter's and put on a pair of these dungaree pants that you couldn't pour a ten-year-old girl into.

When my sugar walks down the street, all the little birdies hold their breaths.

For reasons unknown to your correspondent, a lady hereabouts feels like a square if there is enough room between her and the pants to slip a thin bill.

There are pockets on these pants. But believe me, no lady dast carry a yo-yo in them. She cannot even carry her lipstick, they are that fast to the skin.

The odd thing is, the Levi was made originally in the 1850's for California gold miners. They had plenty of pocket room. So a miner might carry his tobacco and likewise squat to swish the mining pan around.

Then the days of gold passed. And the Western lady visitors took these pants. They sloshed them in bleach and shrank

174

them. And by and by, it became so fashionable that when a lady comes in to buy a pair these days, they just lift them out of the boys' department. And voilà! There goes madam down the street. And where madam goes, the pants aren't far behind. I kid you not.

MEXICO

"Poor Mexico," said President Porfirio Diaz. "So far from God, so near to the United States."

The American tourists are down here in full force, escaping the winter cold that blankets the American cities.

We look out on a dark plaza with little trees. It is lit by little round lights that look like small golden moons floating in the dark. The yellow glow of the church tower clock rides in the dark heavens.

Poor Porfirio! He fled aboard ship from this very port. One jump ahead of a firing squad. That was in the old days. Before the tourists came.

Us on a bus

I was lying around Phoenix, Arizona. Soaking up the expensive resort sun and reading the comics and the lost-and-found ads and such, when I ran across:

18-DAY ALL-EXPENSE TOUR
SEE ROMANTIC MEXICO
ALL FOR $198

And naturally since I am no man to resist a bargain, I must dust down and purchase a ticket. Ole!

"Is it truly romantic?" I asked the busman. For it turns out that this is a Greyhound bus operation.

"Is it romantic?" he said, leaning across the counter in a confidential way. "Bullfights! The canals of Xochimilco! Tropical nights under the coco palms!"

"I do not wish to fight any bulls," I said, "nor to have any bulls mad enough to fight me. As for canals, I went through the Panama Canal once and wondered why they dug it so deep.

"I have just done a number of tropical nights in the Fijis," I said. "And am so full of coconut milk I gurgle when I run."

"There are also romantic señoritas of Old Mexico," said the busman briskly. "Dark eyes flashing under lacy mantillas. Coquettes behind fans. Need I say more?"

"You need not," I said. "One round-trip ticket, if you please. I will ride the canals and fight the bulls. And if a dark eye should flash behind a mantilla, I will flash back, polite as butter."

The once-a-week tours leave from Phoenix. One week they go down the West Coast through Nogales and return the central route through El Paso. The next week they are reversed.

There were 32 people on my tour.

"We will now play a game," said the busman as we rolled south through Arizona. "We will play 'What's My Line?' "

He then marched the first man up to the front seat.

"Your name and address, please? O.K. We will now guess your business."

"What business do you say?" said the busman to me.

"President of U.S. Steel?" I said shyly.

The next lady guessed he was a paving contractor. I do not know why. Possibly he looked a little dusty and she figured he had just come out of a sack of cement.

Finally, after much guessing, it turned out he was a retired carpenter.

As this game progressed, we discovered two mathematics teachers—very handy companions if you were doing your income tax. A Michigan lawyer. A sawmill operator. A fisherman. A retired sea captain. And so on.

I was not riding under my square name. For if you write for papers, your companions either freeze up on you, or else they begin to tell *you* how to write. Or they figure you have such a snap they want you to tell *them* how to write.

I gave them my queer name. And after much guessing admitted that I was a breeder of tropical fish.

This has set me up considerably in the tour. And by the time

179

we crossed at the dusty border town of Nogales, one lady had already engaged to have a long heart-to-heart talk with me about fish.

Safety last

The fine thing about traveling in Mexico is that all us fearless tourists expect to get sick. Fearless, but sick as a dog.

"You should not drink the water," said the tour guide. "You must call the hotel desk and ask for purified water. Agua purificada."

"Agua purificada," we chorused obediently.

All our tour passengers then dug in their purses and verified that they still had their little bottles of pills. We all carry them. For no visitor comes to Mexico without the most awful warnings from friends:

"Don't drink the water or eat the salads."

It is mighty fine to go flying down the highway with the Aztec tummy-ache lying in ambush at every corner.

People who do not get the tourist problem really feel cheated. I think most of them don't get it. But by and by with a little thought, you can raise a mild flutter in the Derby Kelly.

If you keep it in mind, by the time you get home you can make it a quick brush with the angels. You too can be an adviser to future visitors.

"Sick? Man I was *so* sick. Now I tell you what to do. You get these pills and—"

One lady aboard our bus got sick just as we crossed through Mexican customs at Nogales. Undoubtedly a record. She suffered bravely but let us know about it. We were envious as all get out.

180

Uno, dos, tres . . .

"Today," said the guide, "we will learn to count in Spanish. Uno, dos, tres."

"Uno, dos, tres," we said.

"Very good," said the guide. "Before you reach Mexico City you will be able to count to one million."

Each day we get a little lesson.

How to count. The airmail postage rates. You should be careful crossing streets because Mexico City taxi drivers dearly love to clobber a pedestrian. If he does a good job, they award him both ears and the tail. Like a bullfighter.

When and where to bargain. What you can and can't eat. And what medicine to take if you make a mistake.

The President of Mexico is elected for six years and cannot be re-elected.

Everybody in Mexico has to vote. You are not punished if you don't vote. But if you have no certificate that you voted, you cannot get a property deed, a marriage license, or a passport.

"Also," said the guide, "Mexicans talk with their hands. If a Mexican waitress holds her thumb and forefinger close together and extended like this, it means, 'Wait a minute.' An elbow on the counter means, 'You're stingy.' "

One finger under the eye, he said, means, "Watch out." A pull at an imaginary beard, "Delicious." May be applied in a flattering way to delicious ladies, said the guide romantically.

"Sometimes you may see two taxis almost crash. One driver will hold up his fist with the thumb and little finger extended. Like this. That means, 'Your wife is running around with everybody in town.' "

181

This is very handy indoctrination. A foreign country is a perilous path to a new tourist. It is handy to know how to say "Wait a minute" with your hands. Or insult a taxi driver.

We are instructed how to tip: 10 per cent of the dinner check, a peso per bag in and out of the hotels. The Mexican peso's value is eight cents.

"Also," said the guide, "be very careful not to step in the updock."

"What is updock?" I asked.

"Nothing's up with me. What's up with you, Doc?" said the guide.

What I mean, we not only get the tour. We get the jokes, too.

The last bus ride I took in Mexico was 15 years ago. The conductor was barefoot and drunk as a lord. After he collected the tickets, he lay down in the aisle and went to sleep.

The driver wore a rakish cap and a white scarf. He had a wide leather belt inlaid with colored glass and was a real flyboy. He took all blind curves on the inside and snatched us from death at the last possible moment.

But bus driving has improved a good deal since those adventurous days.

Our driver drives with caution. He does not look on burros and pedestrians as a target for tonight. He keeps to the outside on curves.

My memory of Mexican buses is that they were equipped with built-in St. Christopher medals instead of brakes. The driver having more faith in the Saints than in General Motors.

Our driver wears a holy medal. But I have a feeling he is not pestering Heaven with more than can be handled.

"Muy moderna"

In Mazatlan I caught one of those little two-seat buggies they call arañas. Seven pesos an hour—56 cents American.

"You like Mazatlan?" asked the driver.

"They have ruined the town," I said gloomily. "Big buildings. Night clubs. It is no longer Mexico."

"We have the highest brewery in Mexico," said the driver proudly.

"It sticks out of the skyline like a sore thumb," I said.

To be honest, the way I remember Mazatlan, it was a very poor town. The hotels had no hot water. Electric lights went off at the worst hours. The restaurant food was awful.

Now the streets are paved. The electricity is reliable. The bath water would cook eggs. There are several good restaurants.

Once I was arrested in Mazatlan. The policeman said I laughed at him. I had just been at the next table when a political gentleman plugged his seat mate with a big .45. Laughing was far from my thoughts. Anyway, the cops put a rifle in my back. They ran me up an alley where I spoke rapidly and politely of the Good Neighbor policy.

I complimented the entire police force and talked of my love for Mexico. I perspired a good deal, too.

We settled matters for three pesos and a good cry on each other's shoulders.

"No more of that," said the driver. "The bite is prohibited for tourists. Too much money comes here."

A number of fine hotels have been built on the Mazatlan beaches. But Mexico does not change overnight. Somehow they manage to engineer them with booby traps.

The doors invariably pinch your fingers. This results from putting the knob too close to the edge. When I am fresh in Mexico, my thumbs stick out like the Mazatlan brewery. I cannot seem to remember.

I close the door and *wow!* However, you can always press doorbells with your forefinger. Mexico makes you philosophical.

Down at San Blas in the jungle country, they built a beautiful semicircle hotel. Somehow they engineered the gentlemen's lounge into the very center of the main floor without ventilation.

This did not stump the management at all. They just cut a great big waist-high window into the kitchen alongside.

It was very interesting and the cooks carried on some lively conversations with the guests. We got to know each other very well.

"In the old days," I said, "there was a ruined fort on the hill. They used to shoot prisoners against the walls."

"No one is shot in Mexico any more," said the driver. "We are progressive. Muy moderna."

"But you still have the horse and buggy."

"Ah," said the driver, "we keep them for you turistas. We have many modern improvements. Coca-Cola. The jukebox. Possibly next year I will buy the taxi. I will learn English and be a guide to rich tourists."

"What will you show them?"

"The new brewery," said the driver.

My old box Brownie

In the cool Mexican morning we all got aboard the bus and set out for Guadalajara and the high country.

"I get about 1/50 at f. 8 this morning," said my seat mate. "No depth of focus!"

"I felt a little peckish myself," I said. "Possibly it was the shrimps."

"The light reading," he said. "For the camera. Don't you take photographs?"

"I buy postcards," I said. "Not being able to fathom out the meters and wave lengths. And all the other gadgets that have been added to these things."

"Why, it is quite simple," he said simply. "Now you see this dial here? Now look through here and—"

I was quite a hand with the old box Brownie. The kind where you looked in the little square of glass and said, "Hold still." Then you pushed the lever and the other person said, "I think my eyes were closed."

When the prints came back from the drugstore, everybody cried:

· "Oh, I look terrible!"

That was photography when it was simple.

Everybody photographs these days. And it is the most wearing thing I ever saw.

First you get a very small camera. "Hardly takes up more room than a pack of cigarettes."

This is very true of the camera. But the things that go with it!

With the pack-of-cigarettes camera we must carry a knapsack big enough to stuff a body into. It contains long-distance lenses, interchangeable film packs, stroboscopic flashlight equipment. Enough bulbs to fill one of those cigarette signboards in Times Square.

Extra fronts. Extra backs. A small boy to hold the extension cord. Filters. Light meters. Just assembling all this gear makes you limp.

At intervals our guide halts the bus and all passengers mount to have at the Mexican scenery. Like a gong to battle stations.

We photograph the distant mountains. We photograph the burros. We photograph the native in his native habitat. The Mexicans along the coast highway have been light-measured so much they can almost tell *you* the correct setting.

"That one oughta come out pretty well," we say climbing back in the bus. "The oxcart moved before I could get set. But the mountains are pretty."

High road to Mexico

From Guadalajara you are in the heart of Mexico. The road climbs through pine forests, rising to the bleak treeless plateau at 9000 feet before it drops into the dusty, antique Valley of Mexico.

It is highly historical. And I was glad the tour stopped at Morelia. I know where there is a million dollars—maybe two million dollars in Morelia. All jewels and gold bars. Spanish stuff.

The guide said we would stop overnight at the Hotel Virrey de Mendoza.

The Virrey de Mendoza was built for the Spanish viceroys in the days when this town was called Valladolid. It has enormous doors faced with decorated cowhide and an inner courtyard with balconied rooms around it.

If you get one of the front rooms, you have French windows overlooking a beautiful plaza. And a canopied bed. It is the kind of bed to get into and dream about treasure.

The waiter brought me a tequila out by the courtyard fireplace under the ancient oil painting of Mendoza.

He brought a little salt and some sliced limes. You lick the salt, sip the tequila and suck the limes.

"There is a good deal of treasure in Morelia, no?"

"Si, señor. Plenty."

"Where would you encounter it?"

"Who knows? The old people hid it."

I said did he know of a treasure buried in a well. About two blocks from the hotel.

"That one? No, señor. You are a treasure hunter?"

"That is my occupation," I said. "That and playing the national lottery. I also put great faith in the cavalry charges at Santa Anita. However, this treasure of Morelia is authentic."

The waiter said politely he hoped I would become rich. I tipped him an extra peso for his good wishes.

I ran into the treasure of Morelia about fifteen years ago. It is in a tunnel leading from the Cathedral to the outskirts of town. The man who told me had been repairing a well with his father. They broke into it.

"But my papa was afraid of the curse. He stopped up the hole with bricks."

"There is a curse on the treasure?"

"Certainly. All old treasures have a curse on them."

That must be true, curse it. I never seem to stop long enough in Morelia to go dig it up.

187

At night, the band plays in the plaza. Boys and girls walk around the plaza—the boys in one direction, the girls in the other. As they pass, the boys pretend to faint. Or they say:

"St. Peter must have lost the keys, for here is a little angel escaped from heaven."

In a street alongside the plaza, the Morelia housewives come down and sell dinners at little tables. They cook over little charcoal stoves. For about a dollar, you can get broiled chicken and peppery enchiladas and refried Mexican beans and roast kid and black coffee.

By the time I finished dinner and watching the little escaped angels and listening to the band, it was time for the canopied bed. And at 6:30 in the morning we were routed out.

So there was no time for me to go and dig up the treasure of Morelia. Though I know exactly where it is. Curse the luck.

Up in the clouds

We climbed over the hills from Toluca and dropped down into the Valley of Anahuac—the City of Mexico 7300 breathtaking feet above sea level.

The town was called Tenochtitlan when Cortez marched across the causeways of the old lake to inform Montezuma that Spain was ready to take over the real estate.

Cortez came in 1521. He rebuilt the city. But that was not his main purpose.

"What we wish," he told the Aztec king, "is the loot, man."

The Aztec king was Cuauhtemoc, Montezuma having passed to his reward with a little assist from the Spaniards. He said they were mighty poor folks.

Cortez then tied him down along with the Prince of Tacuba. The Spaniards burnt their feet a little to help their memory.

188

"Better tell, King," said the Prince. "For to tell the truth, my feet are getting mighty warm."

"Do you think I am in my bath?" said the King.

This is the first recorded joke in the Americas. It also shows the Spaniards brought the modern hot foot long before Hollywood thought of it.

Mexico City sits up in the clouds. The air is so thin that tourists pant up and down stairs. Planes land at high speeds to keep from stalling out in the transparent air.

It lies in a bowl of hills, beneath the great volcanoes. It has become an international city. Filled with continental restaurants and elegant hotels. It has a greater traffic problem than midtown New York.

And I, who cried out against the long siesta and brought my North American ways here once, now perversely cry out against progress.

"It wasn't like this in the good old days," I told a friend in Del Prado's Montenegro bar the other night.

The friend was Don Keating, a top public relations man.

"What do you mean?" he said, as he ordered double Scotches for us. "These are the good old days."

It is a wonderful country. I have more trouble in Mexico and more fun in Mexico. I am more confounded by habits and customs. I confound more people by my habits and customs.

Mexico rises early. It rises to cockcrow. For the town is filled with fighting roosters and general men-about-the-hen-yard.

The Cadillacs of the políticos roll down the beautiful Reforma. Between the shade trees and past the brooding statues of Mexico's men of antique greatness.

The Indians come in through the back streets with burro-loads of firewood from the mountains.

The new ways and the ancient ways mesh in a crescendo of auto horns and burros braying.

Not all has changed. The tourists still go down to Sanborn's for breakfast in the House of Tiles.

The telephones are still irritable to gringo touch. Electricity has a way of running out for a short beer. Which is why some hotels put a spare candle by the bed.

The siesta hour is almost forgotten. Lunch starts at 2 o'clock. Dinner is after cocktails and cocktails may be almost anytime. An invitation to an 8 o'clock cocktail party means you may show up at 11 or thereabouts without apology.

If you show up at 8, the host may not be home yet.

Señorita Luck

A short time ago, Mr. Dario Borzani came out of a Sears store in the capital packing a chair on his back.

You should remember Mr. Borzani in the dance team of Dario and Diane. Or as the owner of La Martinique in New York. Nowadays, Dario runs the Rivoli, probably the plushest and best restaurant in Mexico.

Mr. Borzani was accosted by a lottery ticket seller. Mexico City is full of raggedy lottery ticket sellers. All insisting on omens and lucky numbers. The tickets come in 20 pieces. You can tear off and buy as many pieces as you like.

"The old lady bothered me so and I had my hands full of chair," said Dario. "Finally I bought five pieces for twenty-five pesos—two dollars American."

Dario was at the bar that night when the returns came in. The first prize ended in seven. If you have the same end number, you get your money back.

"I'll get my money back," said Dario tossing out his five tickets.

"Santa María!" said the barman looking it over. "The first prize!"

"It was $20,000," said Dario. "The old woman offered me both series on that number. If I had bought it all—$80,000!"

Stories like this keep Mexico's Lotería Nacional going at top speed three days a week.

That night Dario closed up the Rivoli and took all the help out in the kitchen. They broke open champagne until morning. All the waiters and barmen who bought tickets all the time, now buy twice as much.

Dario buys them by the bundle.

I buy them myself.

We buy them by dreams. We buy them if they add up to the age of our birthday. We buy them on hunches according to the numbers of the bus we rode.

Top of the week is the million-peso first prize. Each piece of the ticket costs 10 pesos or 80 cents. But if you are a hunch player, you go for the whole 10 pieces at $8.

There is always the chance of gathering in one of the smaller prizes which run into fair money. There are so many prizes that it takes nearly a quarter page to run them in the newspapers.

The profit on the Government lottery goes to schools and hospitals and such. So you can really feel that it is a matter of charity. Income tax is small in Mexico. But if you win, the Government takes 15 per cent.

The other night I spilled a glass of mescal. The barman hastily dipped his finger in it and touched himself behind the ear. So did the cashier. He urged me to do the same.

"The very greatest luck," he said. "Buy a lottery ticket immediately."

"Have you ever won in such a case?"

"Once I came within two numbers. My heart almost stopped. It is a well-known fact that a poor Indian from Chalco won the million-peso prize after spilling three drinks. He was so drunk," said the barman, "he spent all his money on the ticket."

"What happened to him?"

"He moved into a great house," said the barman, "and stayed drunk. Spilling drinks and staying drunk. A happy man. However," said the barman, "he died of drink shortly afterward. You cannot push luck too far."

The pig in the penthouse

The Monte Cassino is a fashionable hotel in a fashionable district. Visiting movie stars stay here. We all live fashionably hereabouts. So it was no surprise when I looked out the window and saw a pig living in a penthouse.

As a matter of fact there are two pigs.

They wander around on the roof and when it gets hot, they have a little shaded balcony. They lie in the shade and cut up touches, I suppose. About other pigs and living conditions.

These pigs are not pets. I suspect they are about to become bacon.

But they do not know this. Any more than we luxury-living people in the hotel across the street can tell when we are to become bacon.

All they know is they are living in a penthouse in a swank district.

All along the highways you run across road signs declaring: *Cuidado con el Ganado.* Look out for the cattle.

This is quite a country for animals. You must cuidado con the cattle and also cuidado con dogs, burros, chickens, pigs and stray horses.

The things you must cuidado wander all over the highways.

Burros cross at a sssssllllooooooow walk. If you hit a burro, the owner gets terribly mad. And it is bad for the burro and bad for the fenders. Cuidado.

Mexican dogs seem to grow to fit the situation.

There is a whole breed of dogs who play the Cárdenas delicatessen in Cuernavaca. They all have the same shaggy sad-eyed look. They sit and eye the tourists eating on the walk across from the Cortez palace.

The tourists are softhearted. They say:

"Oh, the poor starved dog." They throw him a cracker.

These dogs are not starving at all. They are simply fitted to survive because they look like they are starving. They are living in a fashionable tourist town and are hog-fat on the inside as a pig in a penthouse.

The dogs go over and sniff the cracker. But they do not eat it. They are waiting for the leftovers of the Serrano ham. Or else they want the cracker buttered.

This makes the tourists furious. Because a dog has no right to look like he is starving and be so ungrateful about charity.

The maid does not know how the pigs got in the penthouse. Or who owns them and is eying them for bacon.

She accepts it as a matter of course that a pig should live on a roof in this district.

"Because there is no room in the street, señor."

In other words, where else would you expect a pig to live around here? Heavenly days, the maid says to herself while dusting, the questions these tourists ask! Ai!

Mexico is a land of surprises, says my guidebook. "One is constantly confronted with pictures of striking beauty. The bend of the road opens on enchantment."

This is a pretty way to put it. I wish I had said that.

The fact is it takes a good deal to surprise me in Mexico any more.

I used to be surprised by an odd arrangement in the plumbing situation. The top of the bathroom water tank is always broken in half. I have seen half water-tank tops from Juarez to Tuxtla Gutierrez. Finally I asked a service station man.

"Why," he said, "thee hahndle ees broken. So you must reach on the eenside to open the wahtair out, no?"

For simple people, simple answers, no?

I mention this only as a curiosity. For Mexico has quite a few things I would like to import. Telephones, for instance.

The Mexican telephone is free. Even on hotel calls. You can phone in restaurants, bookstores and official offices. No charge.

There may be some difficulty in getting the number. For the Mexican phone is temperamental. In Mexico City, the numbers come in sizes. The dial must be manipulated firmly and slowly.

Mexico had two separate systems. Mexicana and Ericcson.

These systems are supposed to be meshed. But the interlock is a delicate thing. For some reason I get Delaware Punch nearly every outgoing phone call. No matter what I dial.

"Is this De Lara Tours?"

"No, señor, Delaware Poonch de Mexico."

There is a buzzer at my room door. This curious buzzer somehow is activated by the elevator nearby.

It buzzes when you push it. It also buzzes when the elevator performs some complicated maneuver which I have not figured out.

It is entertaining, in a way. Because sometimes you say "Come in." And somebody comes in. Other times. Nothing. Today I said, "Come in." Three men came in and rolled up the living-room rug and went out with it.

I used to ask questions about things like this. Now I just let things happen in my hotel room. They do, too. There is a man who washed down the outside balcony each morning. Today, for reasons I do not inquire into, he took the hose and pointed it down into the street for about five minutes. I never found out why.

The valet may come in late with the pressing. But he brings a whole vase of flowers.

"Ah, but these are not my pantalones."

"Not yours? How unfortunate."

"Very. Do me the favor to look for my own trousers, eh?"

"Immediately, señor. In the little now."

Room service arrives with four bottles of ginger ale and one drink of whiskey, it seems.

"Thanks, but I ordered nothing."

"But, señor, it says here Four Roses."

"Not for me."

"Keep it anyway," says room service philosophically. "We await the other call." Nothing much surprises him, either. He was born in Mexico.

La gripa

It was a sunny Sunday when I showed up with a fashionable illness. At home we would say a cold. Here they say "la gripa."

195

I woke up feeling bad and slightly feverish.

The waiter came up with breakfast. He said what I needed was a virtuous drink of his own country in Oaxaca.

"You take a glass of mescal, hot. Soak cactus candy in it. Drink. Mejor que Penicilana," he said. "Better than penicillin."

It sounded like a local version of rock-and-rye. I said I thought I was not long for the world anyway. And mescal and candy hot would probably finish the job early.

"Lemons, then," said the waiter. "Squeeze Mexican lemons in hot water."

"You drink it?"

"Soak your feet in it."

I worked over a little coffee and lay around reading Madame Calderón de la Barca. The wife of the first Spanish Minister spent two years here in 1840. She wrote a vivid series of letters *Life in Mexico.* As good or better for the tourist than they were then. But she was a healthy woman and I could find no remedy while I coughed gloomily.

After a while the maid came in. She said they have a cure in her country around Acapulco.

"You must bind onions to the soles of your feet with red flannel."

"Why red flannel?"

"It is a holy color. The onions draw out the infection."

It occurred to me I could send down for a hamburger and take the onions off that. But I was poorly equipped in the red flannel line.

The boy who waters the plants on the balcony came by.

He said it was the airs. You must stay out of the airs or get in serious trouble. That is why the Indians cover their mouths and noses with the serape in the cold of the morning.

"Tequila is a good cure."

"Hot or cold? With lemons on your feet? With red flannel? How?"

"Straight," said the water boy. "Natural."

The maid said this did not really work unless you took a teaspoonful of hot sauce with it. "Salsa picante pura."

"Or possibly we could get a curer. A bruja. A witch."

"Are there witches in Mexico City?"

"Plenty, señor. They take away the bad luck."

She said it was not easy to get one in this neighborhood of decent people. You had to go to the outskirts. To the wise Indians.

"If you have somebody who makes bad talk about you, you take a toad and sew its mouth shut. Sew it with green thread. Leave it on their doorstep."

Personally, if I saw a toad with its mouth sewed with green thread, I would not only stop talking. I would stop drinking.

After a while the waiter rang the bell. He said he could find no cactus candy but had brought me a glass of mescal and some lemons and salt anyway. "Just in case."

And sure enough, after a time I *did* feel better. Better than any penicillin I ever tasted.

Man from Manhattan

The former Mayor of New York and later Ambassador to Mexico, Mr. Bill O'Dwyer, lives in a small penthouse apartment on top of the Hotel Prince. Comfortable but by no means luxurious. He had a cold, a box of Kleenex and a bottle of Scotch.

"Do you know there isn't a bookie in Mexico City?" he said. "And I'll tell you why and this is what I told them in New York.

"The city gets so much revenue from the tracks. You can't set up a gambling operation if the city gets it up first. That is what I tried to tell them in New York. Nobody had the nerve to tell them that. But I told them.

"Stan, you can't stop graft in a police department if you've got a bookie on the corner. I don't care what you do. Then pretty soon what have you got? The newspapers full of payoff headlines.

"Anyway, the big city is through.

"You take traffic and all that. The decentralization. Well, the business moves out and you say 'fine.' But when the budget comes up, where are you going to get the billion dollars in taxes they took with them?"

The penthouse opens up on a little patio, looking over the lights of Mexico in the transparent air of nearly 8,000 feet.

O'Dwyer is practicing law in Mexico. He studied at the ancient university in Salamanca in Spain. He speaks good Spanish.

I said I had lunch in the big square at Salamanca this spring.

"A beautiful place," said O'Dwyer. "Did you notice that on one of the gates they have a carved head of Cortez? He was a student there but he had to run to Cuba. Maybe something with a girl. He was a great ladies' man, Cortez. They don't write it in the history books but that he was.

"There isn't a statue to Cortez in all Mexico," said O'Dwyer looking out across the city.

Mexico has turned sharply away from the Spanish—the gachupines they called them, "the spurs." The other day a parade of Indians from far down the coast marched into town.

They marched down the Avenida de la Reforma to the big statue of Cuauhtemoc. Last of the Aztec emperors. They danced and laid wreaths on the statue.

"Been in New York recently?" said O'Dwyer. We said we had been in New York and seen Red Smith and Irving Hoffman and the Kriendler brothers at "21."

"How are they doing?" asked O'Dwyer.

In the little apartment, O'Dwyer has framed and hung his medals. The ones they gave him when he was a Brigadier General in Italy. The ones he got while he was Ambassador. He had his shirt collar open and kept reaching for the Kleenex. He said he didn't want any of the Scotch.

"You take one. Where did you eat in New York?"

We said we ate at the Stork and at Moriarty's Chophouse at Sixth and 52nd.

"I don't remember a chophouse at Sixth and 52nd," he said. "I used to live at 53rd. Well, I haven't been back for a while. You know a couple of sharp boys came down and tried the bookie thing. The Mexican cops said 'Get!' You can't disturb a police department if the city runs the gambling. I tried to tell them in New York. Nobody else would tell them."

He saw us to the door and said thanks for coming up.

"Good night, General," I said.

"Good night," he said. "Give my regards to the Press Club."

Place of no name

In the interests of science, I should report that the world's only known cure for the common hangover is served at one place in Mexico City.

It is served at 9 Xolotl—pronounced to rhyme with "show total." When the taxi driver looks blank, you tell him, "The place where they serve pozole. Behind the Cine Cosmos."

The place with no name has been operating 20 years. It is open only Saturday afternoons and Sunday mornings. Sun-

199

days from 7 to 10 A.M. If you cannot get up by then, they figure you are too far gone to bother with.

While we waited for the pozole, the maestro brought out little glasses of white mescal and some limes and salt.

"This is part of the cure?" I asked.

"Certainly. Mescal goes with pozole."

Mescal itself would cure the common cold. Like tequila, it comes from the spiky century plant. It comes out about 90 proof. But deceptive.

In each bottle of mescal, they drop a worm from the maguey plant. It gives the mescal flavor, they say.

This is not as bad as it sounds. Maguey worms feed on the cactus and are fried sometimes and served like peanuts. The plush Pavillon in New York has them in cans.

For a number of years I have been coming to Mexico without discovering this remarkable pozole cure. Only five pesos, 40 U.S. cents the soup bowl.

Pozole is a corn-base dish from the southern State of Guerrero.

Politicos, cab drivers, generals and laundrymen come to the place with no name on Sunday morning to wipe away the night before.

"And why do they come Saturday afternoon?" I asked.

"To prepare for the next day, señor."

He said it would take a few minutes to dish up the pozole. In the meantime, have another mescal. Everybody at my table was feeling better already. It is a remarkable cure—curing you even before you start.

In the interests of the Good Neighbor policy, the señora came out of the kitchen and gave me the recipe. (She soaks her corn in lye and washes it. But I think you could use canned hominy.)

200

Cook 4½ pounds of fine-chopped pork meat with 6½ pounds of strips of pig jowls about four hours in a little water. Add 4½ pounds of hominy and salt to taste. Let it warm up and serve in soup bowls with plenty of the soup from the pork.

On top of this sprinkle chopped onion. A few pinches of oregano. A pinch of red chili powder. Squeeze in a half a lemon. Lay on top a half dozen sardines and a half dozen strips of avocado.

The señora gave this recipe in kilos, a kilo being 2.2 pounds. When I worked it out, it seemed like a good deal.

"This must cure many hangovers. This is the recipe for your kitchen?"

"No, señor!" she said. "Just for the average family. About ten persons."

I don't know how it is in your family. But if I had a family of ten persons, I would consider it more than average. And if they all had hangovers—well, man!

The Ides of March

Yesterday a raging dust storm swept down on Mexico City. A violent yellow blast as if outraged Aztec gods breathed maledictions from the skies.

This is my last day in Mexico City. I walked down in the Calle Donceles in the old Spanish city.

It is a wonderful part of town, with great antique doors leading into gloomy courtyards. The old prison of the Inquisition where confessed heretics marched out with tolling bells and hooded priests to be burned in the Alameda. (Sam Houston of Texas was a prisoner here.)

The great stone buildings of the Conquistadors. Carved

saints high in the corners. And for cornerstones, carved serpents from the Aztec temple.

The street of Tacuba, where Cortez retreated on the Sad Night.

The street of guitars.

The sunlit squares and the fountains. The letter writers under the portales. Ancient typewriters clacking to the painful dictation of a barefooted Indian.

I must say that this is a love song to Mexico. With the plumbing that is constantly out of order. But people who will walk three blocks out of their way to put you on the right path.

With mañana promises that never come to pass. But a history of battle for freedom that has been going on for 400 years.

I like the lights of the evening on the beautiful Reforma. The noise of the lottery sellers. The scramble of taxicabs around the circular glorietas. (Taxi drivers don't get mad here. They just drive twice as madly.)

I like breakfast on the Bamer roof on a clear day. When you can see far across the old dusty lake bed to the snowy volcanoes.

Or eggs rancheros on a tortilla in the soft light of the old courtyard at Sanborn's in Madero.

When the great Negro fighter Jack Johnson was a guest of a Mexican general in here, the officer coldly laid two pistols on the table.

"Since, as you say, these tourists never eat with Negroes in their own country," he told the manager, "how do they know they don't like it? Everybody sit down, please."

I went up to the Majestic roof garden that looks across the great square to the presidential palace, built by Spanish viceroys.

202

Maximilian made a brief and glittering Emperor there.

Benito Juarez died there. Patriots were murdered in the Empire rooms. Scott's American marines stood guard at the entrances in 1847.

Once 20,000 revolutionary cavalrymen filled the square. Indians in white pajamas with crossed bandoliers and carbines slung across their saddles.

On the night of the 16th of September the President of Mexico rings the bell that hangs in the cupola and gives the "grito" that raised Mexico in a country town.

"Liberty and Independence!"

The dust storm came up like a yellow haze. The wind came down off the mountains above Texcoco, picking up the salty dust on the great flat lake bed. It blotted out the sun and the room was filled with a hazy, yellow light.

Out on the streets everybody pressed handkerchiefs to their faces.

Powdery dust hung in the air of the room and the waiters rushed around mopping off tables.

But by nightfall it began to clear. And out of the sky came a torrent of clearing rain. The black streets reflected pools of light, and I went over to Loredo's Colonial for green enchiladas and red wine from Rancho Viejo.

Walking home under the dripping sky and a piece of lottery ticket on the million-peso drawing in my pocket. With the sight and smell and feel of Mexico, the little streets and plaza and the lighted boulevards all around me.

"Pulque will cure it"

Pulque is a milky sort of brew that comes from the Mexican century plant. It is sold in special bars called pulquerías. And I should say these are places where the tourist never goes.

Nevertheless, it is a very historical drink, having been brewed by the ancient Aztecs. They had 400 pulque gods. The most famous one was Tepoztecatl and he lived in a temple on the hill above Tepoztlan.

I drove over there from Mexico City to see what was brewing in these days of the dry martini era.

There was not much doing, since it was the noon hour. But it is a pretty town. With a shady plaza and a great, gray stone church of much age.

It takes about two hours' climb to reach the temple of Tepozteco. There is a Christian chapel there. The Spaniards were forever climbing hills and tossing down Aztec idols.

The Spanish are reported to have taken captive a number of pretty Indian ladies in this town. But they must have taken them somewhere else. The ladies selling beans and onions and fruit in the open-air market were very colorful. But—well.

One of them asked me if I was a turista. I said yes, a turista and writer.

"Everyone comes to Tepoztlan to write," she said. "Many people."

This is true. Mr. Stuart Chase and Mr. Oscar Lewis and the man who did the study called *Middletown, U.S.A.* They all wrote about the town.

I asked the lady, "How is the pulque, lady?"

She said all the pulque belters were at that moment belting the stuff right across the way. There was a dark little bar with several horses parked in front of it and a lot of booming juke-box music rolling out the door.

It did not look like the Stork Club. But I went over and a gentleman in a serape came out and hung onto my neck and

204

asked affectionately what he could do for me in the little now. I asked him how I could get to Ahuatepec.

When Cortez was marching through this back country, he headquartered for a few days in Ahuatepec. It is said there was a fine garden there.

The gentleman with the pulque said he would point the way to Ahuatepec surely. And in the little now he would accompany me. To the very gates of the village.

He waved a hand in the general direction. Whereupon another Indian came out and said, No, certainly it was in a different direction.

They went into a great argument about it. They hung on each other's necks and shouted and blew pulque fumes at each other.

"Why do you want to go to Ahuatepec?" they asked.

I am not too sure how Mr. Cortez rates after all these years. Not too good in some parts. And perhaps they had heard the story how the Spaniards took away all the Miss Mexicos of 1521.

"To see a garden."

"The gardens of Ahuatepec are nothing. Come to our town of Jojotepec. See the cornfields."

"I would be happy to see beautiful Jojotepec. But I must call on a sick friend."

"Who is your friend?"

"Pedro García." (Show me a town without a Pedro García.)

"We do not know him. Have a pulque with us."

"What a pity. I have an infirmity of the stomach."

"Pulque will cure it."

I shook hands all around and managed to get out. On the way from town we passed the great rocks where Cortez and his soldiers climbed to fight the people of the pulque gods.

205

"Then the people of nearby towns came to make submission," says Bernal Diaz, the historian, "bringing us jars of the wine of the country."

Probably hanging on their necks and inviting them to come to Jojotepec, too.

I can get it for you wholesale

From Oaxaca I went to the little town of Mitla in the Zapotec Indian country.

Mitla is translated roughly as "The City of the Dead." But when I arrived the fiesta of San Pablo was starting. And the little town along the river was quite lively.

A traveling fair had set up its whirling rides. And most of the Indians were belting home brew and throwing rings to win celluloid dolls. A bullfight was programed for the afternoon and small boys chased through the rough dusty street crying:

"Pyramids, señor! I show!"

"Beat it," I said. "Andale."

This turned out to be quite a mistake. Most of Mitla's streets cross the river. Between fences of planted cactus. The road wrenches your car painfully. But if you get a boy to show you the way, he will take you over a bridge.

Mitla gets its name from the pyramids where Zapotec kings and priests were buried. It is pure Zapotec and the walls are encrusted with zigzag designs.

Only one pyramid is in good shape. The Spaniards tore down the others and used the stone to build the great church that stands just back of the ruins.

They limed over the walls of surrounding buildings. A few

years ago, the lime was knocked off. And now the church is surrounded by the original designed walls.

There were Mitla women all around the church and they rushed over with baskets of carved Indian figures.

"Antiques! Antiques! Buy, señor! Cheap!"

"Made by hand or by machine?" I asked.

"Antique, señor. Puras antiguas!"

They were persistent. Some of the figures had been antiqued. But many of them were fresh from the village factory. One lady offered ash trays carved with Mitla designs. They were perfect tourist souvenirs and needed only a carved *Memories of Mitla* on them to compete with the pine-stuffed pillows of Niagara Falls.

"The ancients used ash trays?" I said.

The lady did not bat an eye. "Yes, why not, señor? Absolutely authentic antique ash trays."

OUT BEYOND THE WEST

HAWAII

The mixture of language is wonderful. The Honolulu *Star-Bulletin* reports a traffic accident:

"Jones was going makai on Kalakaua boulevard while the other pedestrians were in the crosswalk going mauka. The car was going ewa."

Directions are not given in compass points but rather in the Hawaiian manner. "Makai" toward the sea. "Mauka" toward the mountains. "Ewa" toward Pearl Harbor. Opposite, you would be "going Diamond Head."

From the Japanese, the Hawaiian picks up "papa-san and mama-san."

"Go for broke" is Hawaiian for "shoot the works."

"Hail, Hail, the Gang's All Here" translates "Banzai, Banzai, Everybody Stop."

"Smot fella! Been to States!"

"Tell me a story," she said. "Very well," I said. "Once upon a time there was a poor, poor man. He had a daughter eleven years old who was a fragile flower of a child. Being able to eat only four or five times a day. And then only hamburgers, pickles and four slices of chocolate cake."

"What did he do?"

"He was a wood chopper. He chopped out sentences on his typewriter and they came out quite wooden.

"One day as this poor man was toiling and slaving, Bernie Clayton from Matson Navigation Company called up. The man said: 'You poor slave, how would you like to turn in your secondhand pumpkin for a big bright DC-7 and go to Honolulu where we are opening the Princess Kaiulani Hotel?' So the poor man got out his pitiful white dinner jacket—"

"You're going to Hawaii! Take me with you, please, please!"

"You wouldn't like it," I said. "I shall have to live off the country. Off coconut cake and mahi mahi and papaya and breast of guinea hen. Jack Fischbeck at the Royal Hawaiian will force champagne down my throat—"

"Father! Please!"

"There will be nothing to listen to but Bill Akamuhou's music. The palm trees will rustle all night and I shall have to listen to the Waikiki surf. With nothing to smell but pikake and white ginger—"

212

"I want to go!"

"It is enough to wear down a strong man," I said. "Let alone a beat-up little old eleven-year-old."

"I *have* to go! You promised once, remember?"

"Smot fella, been to States!" I said. "Which is to say, you think you're smart, don't you? I do not remember any such promise. However," I said, "I happen to have a half-fare ticket—"

"I *love* you," she said. "You speak Hawaiian beautifully."

"Naturally," I said. "All kine langwidge you fada spik. Him spik French, Texas, Brooklyn, Hawaiian. All kine. Plenty smot fella! You catch new drass, Five-Ten store. We go for broke. Which is to say, shoot the works," I said. "Anything up to five dollars."

United Air Lines first-class DC-7 leaves San Francisco at 9:30 in the morning. It is a plush flight with a red-carpet entrance and Hawaiian music piped over the plane's loud-speaker.

The plane was loaded with Matson brass, presidents, vice-presidents. The Princess Kaiulani opening was one of the biggest things that ever happened to the islands. We were hardly off the ground when the stewardess was around with champagne. Coca-Cola for children.

"I thought you said I wouldn't like it," she said.

"Well," I said, "it's only New York State champagne. Anyway, aloha!"

"Can I stay all summer? I need a new bathing suit."

"You cannot stay all summer. Also you did not tell me you needed a new bathing suit. When you were conning me into taking you, you said it would cost practically nothing. You said you would not plaster me with purchases. Nor go out over your head unless I was with you.

"In fact, there were many promises I seem to remember when this trip was in the balance."

"Just the bathing suit," she said. "I'll never ask for *anything* else."

Well, that was this morning. Exactly eight hours after leaving San Francisco, the DC-7 slid over Waikiki. With the pink Royal Hawaiian and the white Moana below. Over the green shallows and on to the airport.

A big brown Hawaiian lady draped us with white flower leis. The Hawaiian guitars poured out music and the palm trees rustled in the tropic air exactly as promised on the brochure.

At 3 o'clock we made the bathing suit buy, got on the beach and got a surfboard. And that is the last I have seen of one eleven-year-old who promised everything, anything. That smot fella. Been to States!

Good old days

After you have been in Hawaii a week and have turned the color of cocoa, you are permitted to sit on the beach at Waikiki and mourn for the good old days.

The good old days were a couple of years ago. "Before the place was overrun with tourists, my dear."

If you cannot remember when it was *not* overrun by tourists, you certainly must remember that it used to get a different class of tourists. If you can remember neither of these, you need more sun tan.

The first tourists came with Captain James Cook, originator of the first Cook's tour. The Captain was working for His Majesty's Navy, gorblime.

214

"It's good real estate," said the Captain. "But I doubt if it will ever get more business than Florida. No hotels."

He advised the natives to go on eating coconuts, stay right with Great Britain and to stop breaking up his small boats for the nails. Nails were very much in demand for fishhooks. If I told you what the present of a nail did to an island girl, you wouldn't believe me.

Naturally that was in the good old days. Today you could throw carpet tacks from here to Kona and get nothing but sore feet. It was different in the old days. Cook's sailors soon found out the ratio of nails to romance. The ships were practically falling apart.

One day the Captain was ashore trying to get a few nails back. This made the chiefs quite annoyed. They belted the skipper on the noggin with a big club.

"You're a sick man, Captain," they said. "We relieve you."

The second wave of tourists were missionaries from New England.

They advised the natives to go to church and for goodness sake, put on some clothes. The natives could not see wearing clothes because they got wet when you went swimming.

"You don't seem to get the idea," said the Hawaiian king. "This isn't Cape Cod, son. This is Hawaii. It's *warm* here."

The missionary wives knew how to handle this problem. They got hold of the Hawaiian ladies.

"Nobody in Paris is wearing the low-cut neckline any more," they said. "It is strictly passé."

The Hawaiian neckline was cut right down to the grass skirt. Mighty soon the Hawaiian ladies were wearing Mother Hubbards. This sacked up some of the best scenery in the islands which disappeared for years until the modern tourists brought it back again in Jantzen boned swim suits.

215

If you ask me, there was very little to look at in the good old days except coconut trees.

Great day in the morning

As of this morning I tucked a hibiscus behind the ear and went down to sneer at the tourists.

This is the sport of Boat Day. Every two weeks the gleaming white *Lurline* rounds Diamond Head, the shore-side rail crammed with a fresh crop. She turns into Honolulu harbor and lays alongside the dock below Aloha Tower. The Hawaiian music pours out from under the shed and the newcomer is up to his nose in flower leis and sentiment.

"This thing comes in four waves," said a long-time island resident. We were standing in the breezy marble hotel lobby watching the arrivals.

The newcomers run a gantlet of old-timers. Like me. We have been here two weeks. Boy, are these malihinis pale! Boy, are we tanned! Aloha!

"First wave is when they arrive," he said. "The problem then is to get their baggage to the room. The baggage is late coming from the ship. Big problem.

"Second wave is one thirty. All the people who were here have to be shipped to the boat. Much aloha. Much music. Much problem with baggage.

"Third wave is four o'clock. Telephones. All the people who have seaside rooms want to be on the mountain side. All the mountain side want to be on the seaside. Lady says she can't nap on account of the mynah birds. Lady says she can't nap on account of the palms rustling. Please shut off the trade winds.

216

"Fourth wave is six o'clock when the hotel throws a guest cocktail party. Much music. Everybody cocktails. After that the hotel management goes home and goes to bed. Every two weeks."

The paradise of the Pacific is a great title but has a backfire. Because people, having paid their money, are apt to demand Paradise. Take the mynah birds.

The mynah birds do not care whether you are sleeping in the $100-a-day suite. Birds of Paradise should be quiet of a morning while the people of Paradise seek slumber.

The mynah birds wake at dawn.

"Hey, fellers," they cry. "Let's wake up the rich folks!"

"Chatter, chatter, chatter, chatter. Hey, hey! Fire! Help! Everybody *up!*"

The mynah birds nested in the great spreading banyan tree at the entrance to the Royal Hawaiian. After explaining for a long time that the mynah birds were not on the payroll and could not be fired, the manager desperately chopped off most of the limbs.

The mynah birds then flew over to the other side of the garden where they now wake up the people on the other side of the house.

There are no mosquitoes in Paradise. The coconut is spread on cakes. The coconuts are carefully picked so that no nut can billiard off a tourist noggin.

For a modest $2 or $3, the malihini can drape himself in orchid leis. The orchids that come up from the Big Island and are sold by the ton. He can tan himself with guaranteed Hawaiian sun. The trade winds blow each day and the air is so clear that every scanning shows a postcard view.

The *Lurline* this morning was filled with a dental convention. Jovial gentlemen who seemed to be looking professionally at your mouth. Ready to say: "We ought to do something about that one."

They come in a little apprehensively. The band is playing in the lobby. And they must run the lines of tanned hotel guests. And how are they to know that all these people are simply waiting to go aboard the same ship and be long gone by sundown.

Isle of romance

Since Hawaii is South Pacific with built-in ukuleles, you would think every evening would be enchanted. Romance would be a surf ride. Not so, said the social director for the Royal Hawaiian.

"These girls come out here on vacation," she said. "Do they come out to tour the monuments? They do not. They come to get a Man."

She said her best advice to the nut-brown tourist maiden briefly is to get in something brief and get on the beach. "At least 90 per cent of the people meet on the beach."

Let me add that all this is highly moral. You just have to have somebody to dance with, don't you?

Onward now to the tale of the Rev. Hiram Bingham.

The Rev. Mr. Bingham came from New England in 1820. He found the Paradise of the Pacific in terrible shape.

"The appearance of destitution, degradation and barbarism, among the chattering and almost naked savages was appalling," he wrote. "Some of our number, with gushing tears, turned away from the spectacle. Others with firmer nerve continued their gaze but were ready to exclaim: 'Can these be human beings! How dark and comfortless their state of mind and heart?' "

The Reverend set about correcting this state of affairs. And the reason I mention it is because it seems to me this was the first social direction.

In these days there was no problem of Boy meets Girl. I suppose everybody knew each other.

The Bingham party advised everybody to be less sinful.

The Reverend got hold of King Liholiho.

"Son," he said, "you sure are a sinful man. In fact," said the Reverend, "you have got enough sin to put a New England meetinghouse into revival just looking at you. Everybody around here is sinful and had better get on the ball before they slide into eternal fire."

The King was very surprised. The only white people he had known were whalers. They never complained about the social setup.

The Reverend sat down with the King and explained about morals and so on.

"So that's what's wrong," said the King. "Well, possibly it is bad. At least for the common people. What do you think I should do?"

The Reverend said the best thing would be to pass a law. When Boy met Girl they should do something serious like getting married. Not just gad about.

The King thereupon passed the law. He also put all the ships in the harbor off limits to the local girls.

The sailors were considerably boiled over the new social direction. Lieutenant Percival commanding the U.S. Navy's *Dolphin* offered to throw a few shells at the royal palace. The King said well, the law would not apply to ships.

He made the law stick on the common people, however,

who did not have cannon. Boys who met Girls were shipped over to do time on the island of Maui. And when you drive to Hana, you will be pleased to know that you are riding on road laid by misbehavior.

The law eventually fell into discard. Otherwise the whole island would have been super-highway.

No trouble at all

In this carefree Pacific Paradise of happy, carefree natives, the happiest is probably Mr. Chick Daniels. Mr. Daniels is the barefoot Sherman Billingsley of Waikiki. Mâitre d' beach boys. King of the sands.

Mr. Daniels, father of five and grandfather of nine, is known as a "beach boy." If you are smart, however, you will address Mr. Daniels politely. The seating arrangements on the carefree sands of Hawaii are as rigid as behind the gold ropes of the Stork Club.

Properly sorted, sheep from goats and presidents from account executives, we lie under the Waikiki sun. And Mr. Daniels anointeth us with sun-tan lotion.

Chick Daniels went on the beach in 1918. He is the oldest member of that tight fraternity of beach boys who give surfboard and ukulele lessons. He has seated diplomats and brushed off brash movie stars to the back row.

In 1950, Chick was discovered by Arthur Godfrey. Apparently he showed the proper amount of humility, for Mr. Godfrey took him to New York, where he appeared for a month among the cake-mix talent.

His true name is William Daniels.

"Long time ago," said Chick, "they have a plantation strike and three of us sign up for guards. Three Bills. Little Bill,

Tough Bill and me. Finally they got to call me Chick because that time they have fellow name Chick was great detective in book.

"Like Turkey. They call him Turkey because he speckle like turkey egg. Panama, he always talk to people: 'I just come from Panama.' No, he never be in Panama, jus' say that, you know."

Chick works for the Royal Hawaiian. But the rest of the beach boys are under the command of the very social Outrigger Canoe Club. There are 12 beach boys. A handsome job with some outstanding tips at times. I was present a few years ago when a grateful customer handed Panama $400. Panama disappeared for a week.

At Christmas and New Year, Chick said, the beach boys give a party.

"Everybody bring a bottle. Maybe 150 people. More people, more bottle. Everybody sing, dance, laugh. Everybody HAPPY! No trouble at all. Start at nine o'clock, stop at one o'clock. Sometime little trouble brewing, but we stop just like that.

"Everybody happy. No trouble. Sometime laugh, sometime cry. But no trouble. Drink, dance hula, play ukulele, whatever you want. Some party!"

Chick said it was no bed of plumeria, however, this catering to the sun-tan set.

"Some people want umbrella up even when the wind blow. O.K. I tell boys, 'Never argue.' They say, 'Chick, I get a bad time.' I go talk those people myself. No trouble at all. Everybody happy."

Chick said next to the New Year and Christmas party, the biggest thing on Waikiki is a beach boy's funeral.

"We take all canoes, big one in center with ashes. We take way out to sea. Sing all his favorite songs. Have service with

221

priest just like in church. We get way out to sea, we sing canoe club song. We throw ashes out to sea, then all come in, fast, fast *race* in! Catch big wave, paddle fast! Back to beach."

Chick said about 15 beach boys are laid away, out there beyond the big combers that carry the outriggers and surfboards in to shore. Most of them Chick knew when—

"Only the Moana here in those days. Every night we go out on the pier. Play music. No charge. Everybody happy. Now more commercial, no music on beach. But no trouble. No trouble at all."

Song for a princess

The plush, 11-story Princess Kaiulani Hotel was opened in Honolulu the other day. A great white wedge of tropical building stitched with curving balconies, set in the coco palms of Waikiki.

The old-time residents said they had never seen anything like the turnout of high Hawaiian families. The coffee-color Hawaiians of older days before the lighter-skinned Chinese, Japanese, Portuguese and Americans changed the color of the islanders.

The Hawaiian societies took over the event. Put on the pageant and wore the feathered leis you see only on great occasions. All because of the name: Princess Kaiulani.

Chick, the major-domo of Waikiki beach boys, told me: "Because it very bad luck not to celebrate her name. You think to yourself maybe—so not really bad luck. No such thing. But then you get to think"—he tapped his head—"and you go."

The celebration was held in the open area by the swimming pool. There were the yellow, torchlike kahilis of Hawaiian

222

royalty. The ritual hulas. Not the night-club hula, but the hula that tells a story of great tradition.

"Wahine Holo Lio," praising Queen Emma, not only as a great ruler but as a skillful horsewoman.

"He Alii No Oe." The song of the people singing to their Alii or chiefs.

"Aka La'i O Kuhiau." Song of the journey of Kuhiau, chief of Kohala.

In the shaded background sat the antique Hawaiian ladies in their high-collared black court gowns of the Eighties. When Kalakaua was King and a very young girl was growing up with the titled name: Princess Victoria Kawekiu Kaiulani Lunalilo Kalaninuiahilapalapa.

The last heir to the Hawaiian throne was born in 1875. Part Scot, part Hawaiian. Her father was A. S. Cleghorn and her mother was Princess Miriam Likelike. She grew up on her own royal estate of Aunahau, a great garden land adjoining the 4½ acres of the new hotel.

She was sent to England when she was fourteen to be educated, returned in her early twenties and died on the island of Hawaii when she was twenty-four. A rheumatic heart was the killer.

It was the aloha of old Hawaii, anyway. Queen Liliuokalani had been deposed. And McKinley signed the bill taking over the islands.

The Robert Louis Stevenson room is on the top deck of the hotel. Looking over the great curve of Waikiki beach and the blue water. Higher than anyone has ever looked from a stationary point over the land below. A well-named room, for it was Stevenson who told the young Princess of Europe where she was going. And wrote for her:

> Forth from her land to mine she goes,
> The Island maid, the island rose,

Light of heart and bright of face:
　　The daughter of a double race.
Her islands here, in Southern sun
　　Shall mourn their Kaiulani gone,
And I in her dear banyan shade,
　　Look vainly for my little maid.
But our Scots island far away
　　Shall glitter with unwonted day,
And cast for once their tempest by
　　To smile in Kaiulani's eye.

Written in April to Kaiulani in the April of her age; and at Waikiki, within easy walk of Kaiulani's banyan! When she comes to my land and her father's, and the rain beats upon the window (as I fear it will), let her look at this page; and she will remember her own islands, and the shadow of the mighty tree; and she will hear the peacocks screaming in the dusk and the wind blowing in the palms; and she will think of her father sitting there alone. R. L. S.

JAPAN

On a lighted gayway in Shinju-ku district, the Japanese were jumping from bar to bar. They jammed the pin-ball pachinko parlors, their breath frosting the glass on the machines.

In the little paper night club, the girls pushed around the only stove. Like a nestful of kittens. From time to time a strip teaser came in and shivered through a number.

She works a whole string of these little night clubs and is known to correspondents as Miss Goose Pimples of 1958.

In the paper-lanterned narrow streets, the painted geisha girls go clackety-clack to their work. With their bright brocade kimonos swishing and the big geisha wig almost unbalancing them.

Old Japanese customs

I flew into Tokyo with a complete Mexican dinner for 10 people. Frozen, dry-iced and packed in the cold belly of a big Boeing.

"I hope you scattered your cigarettes through your luggage," said the Pan American man at the airport. "Japanese customs are tough on cigarettes right now. But they only charge duty on what they actually see."

The Japanese Customs man looked at the luggage and then at me.

"Open please."

I stalled with the lock until the baggage boy lifted the two boxes of Mexican food on the counter.

"How many cigarettes you have?" The Customs man drew in his breath politely at the end of each sentence. "Hiss."

"No cigarettes in the boxes. Only tortillas."

"Tortiras?" Hiss.

"And tacos. Also a few enchiladas. All cooked. All frozen."

The Customs man turned to my bags. "You have cigarettes in baggage?" Hiss.

"Just enough for my personal needs." (I had five cartons stacked together. If he would only stay on the food—) "Also in these boxes are a few bottles of salsa picante."

"Where food come from?"

"Papagayo Room. San Francisco."

226

"Ah, so." Hiss. "No fruit, no nuts, no plants?"

"Not a one."

The Customs man dipped into a bag and pulled out a handful of uncooked, fresh chilis. Obviously the Papagayo Room had put in some added starters. I tried to get the Customs man back on cigarettes.

"I have cigarettes in the bag," I said quickly.

"Is a plant, ne?" said the Customs man jiggling the peppers. He dumped them on the counter. Hundreds of them! So it seemed.

"Shall I show you the cigarettes?"

The Customs man called over the chief Customs man. They poked through the green, uncooked chilis. Like Customs men all over, they were delighted with such a problem.

"Plants, fruits, nuts cannot come in Japan."

"I have five cartons of cigarettes here," I said desperately unzipping the cover. "I wish to make a free and voluntary confession and—"

"Maybe have nuts and fruit, too?" Hiss.

"Just the chili peppers, I swear—"

"Must have conference," said the Customs man. He went over in a corner and began to thumb through a Customs book. Probably titled, *Ways and Means to Rack Foreigners Smuggling in Chili Peppers.*

At this point I hoped Customs would take a great, big, hot bite of a chili pepper. I saw 10 Mexican dinners confiscated. The Customs man and the Customs chief came back. They looked sad.

"Where plants come from?" Hiss.

"From San Francisco." Hiss. Hiss me, I will hiss you.

"Plants not allowed come in Japan," said the Customs man.

"O.K. Take them away."

"Except these plants from San Francisco," he said. "Plants from San Francisco, O.K."

"Thank you! Thank you!"

"Now," said the Customs man with a small smile, "you bring plenty cigarettes."

"Just enough for myself," I cried.

"Only 200 piece allowed without duty," said the Customs man. "That will be 2900 yen, please. Maybe about eight dollars American money. You change money over there. You pay here. Thank you so much. Ah, so." Hiss. Hiss.

"Mr. Derrarrprane-san"

I checked into the Nikkatsu, the newest and most modern hotel in downtown Tokyo. The Nikkatsu is an office building with two floors of hotel. The only thing Japanese about it is the accent.

To my room boy, I am "Mr. Derrarrprane-san."

I went out and got an 80-yen taxi. Taxis run on meters. You spot them by a yellow license plate. Little taxis start at 60 yen. Bigger taxis are 80 yen. The ones you and I can get into without bumping our heads are 100 yen. The yen runs 100 to 28 cents U.S.

"Tokyo Correspondents' Club," I said.

"Ah, so," said the driver hissing politely.

We drove around quite a while.

"Tokyo Correspondents' Crub?" he said.

"So, ne?" I said. "Shimbun Alley No. 1. Shimbun Club."

"Ah, so," he hissed.

The Correspondents' Club is four blocks from the Nikkatsu. But I hadn't an idea which way. It was obvious the driver didn't either. He kept stopping alongside parked taxis and carrying on conversations. Everything wound up "Ah, so." Then we went on again.

It is practically impossible to find an address in Tokyo. Taxi drivers navigate by guess and by God. Like Columbus.

There is a good reason. Tokyo is divided into districts. About as big as a Chicago ward. Each district is divided into subdistricts. As near as I can see, street names mean nothing. Most are not named anyway.

Each house is numbered. You know how it is numbered? It is numbered in the order it was built.

If we are looking for 187, 2-chome, Kamiogikubo, Suginami-ku, we do this: We start with Suginami-ku district. We find Kamiogikubo subdistrict.

Now we look for 2-chome, the No. 2 block. Now we try to find the 187th house that was built in the district.

It does not matter that some houses—say 134 and 152 and 154—were torn down. A new house built on the property does not take the number of the previous house. No sir, it gets a new number in rotation.

This makes it a rare occasion when you can find a house with only an address to go on.

The easiest way is to mail a postcard: "Please telephone me." The mailman for 2-chome finds the house. He learns the district like a paper route.

I began to wonder if we would run out of gas. I hailed a couple of Air Force lieutenants. They said they didn't know where the Correspondents' Club was. But—

"Driver-san, you go Officers' Club up there. Ask doorman."

"Ah, so," said the driver.

The doorman was not sure.

We stopped two Japanese policemen. They thought it was in one direction.

A taxi driver came along and hazarded a thought that it was in another.

We drove up one alley. We drove down another. We ran into a one-way street.

"You go Cherry Crub?" asked the driver hopefully. The Cherry Club is a dance spot filled with Japanese hostesses.

"Correspondents' Club," I said firmly.

"Ah, so," said the driver despondently.

We drove up another street and turned into another alley. And there, so help me, there it was.

The driver pulled in with a flourish.

"So, ne?" he said triumphantly.

"Ah, so." I said handing him 200 yen.

Columbus got quite a hand for hitting America. All he had to do was sail west. I wonder what he would have done if the compass had read 29, 2-chome, Hamacho, Nihonbashi Chuo-ku.

No white rabbit?

In New York a couple of months ago, I was talking to Mr. Bob Gibson, the AP man just in from Japan.

"This Nikkatsu Hotel has a ghost of a white rabbit," he said.

"This is bad?" I said.

"Very bad," said Mr. Gibson. "First week they opened the building, one of the airlines in there had a bad crash. Everybody in Japan said that was what came of fooling around with property with white rabbit ghosts."

"What about the white rabbit?" I asked the room boy.

The room boy said, "Ah, so?" He said he never heard of such a thing.

230

I did not move out of the Nikkatsu because of any white rabbits. I moved because I think Japanese-style hotels are better. In Japan.

While I was checking out, I asked if I could go up on the roof and take a look at Tokyo. They said it would be difficult. But finally I found a guard who said he would take me up.

It was an excellent view. And the lower terraces of the building had wonderful little Japanese gardens.

"Have you seen any white rabbits?" I said.

"Ah, so," said the guard.

I was really about to write off Mr. Gibson and his Alice-down-the-rabbit-hole stories. But never underestimate the Associated Press.

Around the corner, I walked right into a little Shinto shrine. It was one of those picture-book shrines. With a stone basin filled with water outside. For you must wash your hands and mouth when you enter.

Just inside the Japanese gate and guarding the shrine were two stone animals.

"Ah, so," said the guard. "White fox."

"Why white fox?" I asked. I thought possibly the AP had given me a white rabbit on the first flash and would correct later.

The guard said a white fox is the fastest carrier of spirit information. If bad luck was on the way, the white fox would carry the news to the owner of the building and let him unload. So, ne?

"Only white fox? No white rabbit?" I said.

"Ah, so," said the guard.

Well, there is nothing like second-guessing your colleagues. I was about to send Mr. Gibson a kite on the matter. But when I turned away I saw something else.

Right on the corner of the building was a great winged gargoyle. He faced north. North where the ghosts come from in Japan. I simply pointed to it.

"Maybe so like white rabbit, so, ne?" said the guard.

I went downstairs and checked out. I have nothing against white rabbits. But my room at the Hirano was only $9. It was $15 at the Nikkatso.

I don't need any white rabbit to tell me $15-a-day is bad luck.

Home is where the floor is

"You writee you shimbun. You newspaper. You writee you catchee Japan clothes. Havee kimono. No catchee pants, so, ne?" said the maid.

I am a doll at my hotel. I am Bob Hope. I am a card. The maids are always dropping in to see what comical thing I am up to now.

When I am in kimono, I am mighty funny. That is what they think. When I am bare I am not funny. Funny, isn't it?

In the morning as soon as I give signs of life the girl-san is in my room. Bustling about and bringing in the hibachi full of glowing charcoal. She hands me the Nippon *Times* and a cup of tea.

After a suitable interval, my bath is announced. I rise and put on an inner kimono of fresh cotton. Over this goes my quilted kimono. There is a cotton belt, freshly washed and rolled up, to tie around the waist.

The bath has two rooms. The dressing room has straw mats on the floor. It has a long washbasin with a willow-stick bottom. My towels are laid out in a straw basket in the middle of the floor.

232

I have two telephones on little 12-inch stands. My shaving mirror is on a six-inch stand. Japanese living is done mainly on the floor.

In the other room the bath steams in the corner. It is wooden. Three feet deep and six feet by four around. A 12-inch stool sits on the plank floor. A little wooden tub full of hot water sits on top of this. There are several faucets on the side of the wall. All about a foot off the planks.

The ritual is something like this: First you climb into the tub. At about this point, the girl-san comes in and reads you the Japanese newspapers. She is very fond of suicides.

"Thisu girl-san likee thisu boy-san, so ne? He papa-san say no can marry. They go Fuji. Catchee medicine tea. Bothee die. Sad, ne?"

"Mighty sad."

"Thisu boy-san takee knife, cuttee self."

Our mornings are very cheerful.

At this point you climb out of the tub. The girl-san empties the little tub of water over the wooden stool and fills it with fresh water. You sit on the stool and she soaps up a towel and begins to wash your back.

It is quite a washing job. Right up to the neck.

When you are thoroughly soaped, she dips the tub in the hot bath and flings several buckets on you. Now you climb back in the tub again.

When you have had enough of this, you climb out and wash your face by filling your bucket at the little floor faucets. You brush your teeth at the faucet.

You soap your face and shave in the little floor mirror.

Now you get back in the tub.

The girl-san said there is a Japanese saying for this luxurious life:

"Boy-san takee bass morning, he likee bed morning, drinkee morning. Before he very rich, you know? Now he no have money."

When you say it in Japanese, it rhymes.

Well, now the bath is over. The girl-san goes away as soon as the soaping is over. We go out in the dressing room. A fresh kimono is folded and waiting. The opaque windows are slid back so that you look on the garden full of fruit trees.

We put on the kimono. We put on the slippers. We go out in the hall.

All the maids laugh so hard they can hardly hold onto their mops. I am a mighty funny shimbun boy. I think they will be sorry to see me go.

A place to sit

In my Japanese hotel, we sit on the floor. We sleep on the floor. We eat on the floor. It is the custom. Custom rules life around here.

Sometimes when the maid is not looking, I go over and sit on the foot-high table. It is a great relief.

I think the maid is watching me.

"When little boy sit on table, his mama scold him. She say, 'You sit on your father's head.'"

We have other sit-down sayings. If life is hard, we say: "You must sit on stone for three years."

Sometimes when I sit on the floor, I am glad it is not made of stone. I can barely stand the straw matting for three hours.

We must eat *all* the rice in our dish. Because—"for each grain of rice, farmer make three drops of water from forehead."

But if we want a second helping of rice, we do not eat all. "Must leave little bit of first rice in bottom of rice bowl."

234

Last night we went to a famous restaurant for actors. They serve exotic food. We tried a bit of the raw snake—it tastes like raw snake, too.

"Making old man feel very young."

I do not feel very young. But prefer the way I feel to a diet of raw snake. Possibly I had an old snake.

When I shop, I must not window-shop. "Must buy something. If you no buy, shop man throw salt on floor when you leave. Keep off bad luck."

The maid who brings my tea calls it "o-cha."

But—"Never speak o-cha in o-sushi house or geisha house." (O-sushi is a rice dish. Geisha house is a teahouse with geisha girl singers.)

"Must say for tea, agari or uji. In these place, o-cha mean no customers."

The fishhouses have a special way of speaking. They bust off the last half of words and sentences. Why? Because, "Mean make business very fast so fish not get old. More fresh."

Now that I can count to 10, I can give my telephone calls in Japanese.

However, I have been doing it all wrong.

"Must not say 'shih' for number four. Must say 'yong.' "

"Shih is not four?"

"Yes, is four. But shih also mean to die. Never say."

There are no number four rooms in hotels. Nor number four tables in night clubs. Neither are there number nines. Number nine is "ku." "Ku means pain."

"How about thirteen?"

"Is O.K., thirteen."

When we go into night clubs, no matter what time, the greeter says "Good morning."

"If say good evening, mean everything close. Must say like start day or very bad luck."

Sometimes I sit on the floor and think about such things. It gives me a great deal of "ku" to sit on the floor. But I would rather "shih" than have the maid catch me sitting on father's head.

The social set

I imagine I am the politest cat in Japan. The entire female staff of my hotel is engaged in improving my barbarian ways.

"Must not walk on tatami in slippers!"

The tatami are the straw mats in a Japanese room. They measure about six by three feet and all Japanese rooms are multiples of the tatami. So we have six-mat rooms, eight-mat rooms and so on.

We take off our shoes at the hotel entrance. (They park them in a little shoe park.) We put on slippers from a row of house slippers. But when we walk into the room, we go in socks.

"Why, lady?"

"Is more porite." I am mighty porite. Poriteness pays.

I sit at a two-foot-high table and can sit sideways if I like. But—

"Girl-san must not sit so. Must sit on feet. For man all right, sit sideways. For girl not porite."

The girl-san must also open the sliding doors sitting on her feet and kneeling. When she comes in, she sits again on her feet and slides the door closed.

If I am introduced, however, I must get off the cushion. Onto the tatami. Then I put two hands on the floor and bow so my head hits the floor.

"Unless introduced to geisha girl. Then she must bow. But you no bow." (I would bow anyway to a geisha girl. I am that porite these days.)

The reason I am so fat with the maid-san is curious.

The other day, Mr. Irving Hoffman, the blade of Broadway, blew into Tokyo. He brought with him an envelope of stills. Moving-picture stars!

The maids flipped! A stack of eight-by-tens of movie stars is better than a stack of dollar bills around here. About six maids hustled up and sat politely on their feet while they shuffled through the pictures.

"Ah, so! Clock Gobble! Very pretty, ne?"

After Clark Gable we are fond of "Aran Lodd." After Alan Ladd, we scream over "Ansony Puckins." Anthony Perkins.

"Everybody wanting Weeyum Hoden." (William Holden was in Tokyo the other night. I had my picture taken with him and showed it to the maids. Wow!)

Mr. Holden changed my whole life. Obviously a cat who hangs out with Mr. Holden is very important. If I kept my slippers on when I am on Mr. Holden's tatami, my maids would simply die.

It would not be porite at all. And Mr. Holden might hold it against them. My maid-san would flip herself out the window with embarrassment.

"Only time when can wear on tatami is when people dead! Then wear geta on tatami." (Geta are the wooden slippers you wear on the street.)

I get orders when I go to dinner.

"You catch dinner Mr. Weeyum Hoden, suppose you like give him somesing from you plate? O.K., must not give him from you chopstick to he chopstick. Not porite! Very bad luck!"

"How do I give to him?"

"Must put in his hand, ne?"

"Suppose I like give Mr. Holden fried egg?"

"Must put in hand."

This is a firm order. And I do hope Mr. Hoden or Mr. Clock Gobble or Mr. Ansony Puckins will forgive me if I chopstick an egg into their hands.

Poor Butterfry

The Japanese lady who served the sukiyaki gave me the lowdown on Madame Butterfly.

"Japanese girl catchee shave oncee week," she said.

"What for?" I said.

"Make mo' pretty," she said. "Japanese girl she go barber. Barber makee shave so." She showed me how the barber shaves the side of the face. "So, makee eyebrow mo' pretty too. Shave so."

Japanese ladies are certainly different.

I wonder where they picked up that title *Poor Butterfly*. Butterfly is Japanese for two-timing.

"Thisu girl, she catchee one boy, maybe so next day catchee new boy. All time changee changee. She butterfry."

The occupation produced a curious occupation pidgin which seems to be understood by everyone. Ladies seem to speak it best. Ladies were more occupied, I guess.

"Takusan" is plenty and "sukoshi" is little. Little in quantity or little in size. A present is a "presento." "Choto mate" is for wait a minute. "Ichi ban" is number one, first cabin. The head of the restaurant or house is either the "mama-san" or the "papa-san."

238

"Nevah hoppen" means not a chance, sailor. Shove off.

The Japanese lady has been more aptly tagged "Baby-san" by Mr. Bill Hume, the artist for *Yank*. He put out a very rare little volume of cartoons on the subject. You buy it for 300 yen.

The other day Mrs. Elizabeth Burdett returned to the States. Mrs. Burdett is president of the American Legion Auxiliary. She said American servicemen marry Baby-san at the rate of 100 a day.

I gather she did not approve of this. For immediately the consul general here came right out and said 100 a week was closer to right.

Whatever the number, it is a cinch that takusan soldiers found Baby-san was mighty cute. And the Japanese ladies knew already what most ladies seem to know. That if you "butterfry" around enough you are almost certain to come up with butter.

Boy-san meets girl-san

"You catchee American house, Chinese food, Japanese wife. Ichi ban. Number one," she said conversationally.

"Yes, ma'am," I said, wiping the soap from my eyes. I am shy as a songbird. Besides I was bare as a radish. It is very hard for me to carry on intelligently without my graduation suit on.

She was a very pretty hotel maid. We had never met before. But I felt as though we were old friends.

A few minutes before she had walked into the bathroom and heaved a wooden bucketful of hot water on me. She lathered me up like a barber. All over.

This is the curious thing about Japan. When boy-san meets girl-san, it is apt to be in the bath.

Oddly enough there is no Japanese word for romantic. In order to get such a word (to go with American movies), they have invented one. Romanticu.

I will tell you about the geisha girl.

The geisha girl is a combination of show girl and companion. It is about like taking a movie starlet to dinner. Only better. The geisha girl spends all evening lighting *your* cigarettes.

My Japanese hotel is in the center of the Akasaka district, famous for the best geisha girls. The girls we can afford are still going to school. Being engaged by us is like playing bit parts.

When they graduate, they will be much higher-priced.

The other night, a Japanese friend engaged two geisha girls for dinner. They arrived in the colorful geisha costume. The doors slid back and they bowed correctly. Not directly toward us but to one side. Heads on the floor and the palms flat with the fingers pointed in a triangle.

It is all done as carefully as a flower arrangement.

But my Japanese friend sent them away. He sent for two others who had a good deal more mileage on them.

"I think the first girls would not please you," he said. "I think they would be clumsy on the samisen."

Well, this is true. If there is anything I cannot stand it is somebody clumsy on the Japanese guitar. I must say that the samisen in any case sounds like a lonely cat on a moonlight night.

I would not want anyone to be clumsy with it.

Some very expensive geishas are grandmas.

You may also engage a geisha boy. The most famous one in Japan now is Bando Motzoguro. He is past his late seventies.

It is like engaging a very famous movie star for a private house party.

The geisha girl is always somewhat available in the romanticu sense. More so when she is young and clumsy on the samisen. When she gets older and better on the samisen, this is not so true.

In this Akasaka district, the geisha is almost purely entertainer.

There are other districts where the geisha schools are not as good. In such places you find what is known delicately as the "pillow geisha."

Even so, the geisha is never exactly what you would call it in the States. She pays a geisha tax and lives with mama-san.

They have the others too in Japan. But they are not geishas.

The hot bath has no romanticu overtones at all. Though it is as social as a dinner. All sorts of people drop in unexpectedly. It is quite an experience to have a bare lady come in, bow, and climb in the same tub.

The tubs are as large as swimming pools. The ladies go on one side and the gentlemen go on the other.

One thing about it, you never know how it will come out. The second day the pretty maid came into the bathroom, I closed my eyes, shyly.

When I opened them again, a boy-san built like a Sumo wrestler had me on the floor and was giving me a spine massage like a pile driver.

"Ichi ban," he said.

"Ah, so," I said. "Take it easy, Jack. This ain't romanticu."

Japanese cookery

The best dinner in the Orient I had at Sukiya-Ryo. Sukiya-Ryo is on a lantern-lighted little street. Half a block from the modern Ginza in Tokyo. I had dinner with Mr. Ken Cole who stayed here for business when the Navy left.

We sat on the floor of course. And I learned about Japanese cooking.

"The secret of Japanese cooking lies in this combination of refinements: Color, odor, flavor, shape and container." So says Isao Yabuki of the Ten-Ichi restaurant in his book on special foods of Tokyo.

I find also that all Japanese meals must contain an odd number of dishes. Never even, except at funerals.

The waitress brings first a steaming-hot towel. You wipe your face and hands. It is surprisingly refreshing.

She brings tea with bean cake and little pots of hot sake. Sake is a rice wine. There is quite a ceremony to it. They pour it in something like a thimble-size egg cup. You take the cup with your thumb and forefinger. Your middle finger goes in the dent in the bottom.

As soon as you finish, she fills it again. And again.

This is apt to put you pretty full of hot sake. The trick is to turn the cup down on the table.

The waitress brought sashimi. The sliced raw fish that you dip in ginger and soy sauce. Then she settled down to the sukiyaki.

Sukiyaki is quite simple. They cook it over a charcoal brazier in a flat pan. You melt butter in the bottom. Put in beef sliced paper-thin. When it is half cooked, you add mushrooms, bamboo shoots and onions. Cook it eight minutes and add sugar, sake, soy bean cake, green onions, gourmet powder and soy sauce.

Everything is laid out with an eye to color and decoration. The waitress kept up a constant conversation. The Japanese believe that you should be entertained while you eat.

"I very lonely," said the waitress. She wore a pretty kimono and handled the cooking chopsticks as though she was arranging flowers.

She pointed to the bamboo shoots and announced that "they make man verrrrry strong."

"Just conversation," said Mr. Cole. "Doesn't mean a thing."

She said that she used all the standard ingredients for sukiyaki. But she also put in pepper, ground red pepper and cinnamon.

After a while Mr. Cole gave her a sake cup. He poured her a cup of sake. Then she poured one for him.

"This means we accept her as a companion," Mr. Cole explained. "We accept her and will talk about the most secret business in front of her."

He said all confidential business is done with waitresses listening. It is part of their tradition that they simply don't hear.

After a while the owner came in and had a cup of sake with us.

Cole said this was a big honor. "When the mama-san has sake with you."

The waitress served the sukiyaki. She gave us each a little cup with a raw egg in it. You beat up the egg with your chopsticks and dip the beef in it.

After you are through, you eat your rice. You pour the rest

243

of the egg and the sukiyaki pan gravy and a little tea over it first. Last, you get your soup. Clear mushroom with a little celery and ginger stick added.

The mama-san sent in three silver dishes. Each had an enormous pair of strawberries with green top still on them, dipped in powdered sugar. You wind up with more tea. And bean cake in a silver lacquered dish.

I have it in my notes: "Best dinner in the Orient." It was.

Tokyo after dark

Tokyo is the biggest booming night-club town in the world. Beside Tokyo, Paris is a quiet night on Main Street, Ohio. My newspaper is filled with ads:

> 100 Beautiful Hostesses Await You
> Eagerly. For Good Time for Everybody
> Come to Club Bangbasha Where You Will
> Forget Your Troubles.

I cannot forget my troubles. But am willing to make the old college try.

The other night we went down to Ginza. Ginza is the main shopping street. But the area back of it is filled with bars and night clubs. Little alleys of restaurants and neons. Japanese paper lanterns and Beautiful Hostesses.

"You like beautiful hostess, sir?" said the headwaiter.

"Could I look first?"

"Better you have beautiful hostess, sir. Very charming. Treating you very nice, sir. Always smiling at you."

A Beautiful Hostess appeared from the bench. They have a bench. Just like a football team. The Beautiful Hostess smiled at me.

244

"You like dance?"

"Why, yes, ma'am. If they will play something slow. A Strauss waltz, possibly. Or if fast, something we can do the Bunny Hug to."

"More better samba," said the Beautiful Hostess smiling. You would think it would crack their make-up. Or their disposition.

We did a little samba. That is, the Beautiful Hostess did a samba. I sort of followed around. Stamping my feet.

"You give 1000 yen, please?"

"What for, ma'am?"

"Hostess no pay. Just get 1000 yen an hour. When get 1000 yen, must pay night club 200 yen."

I gave the Beautiful Hostess 1000 yen. About $2.75 U.S. It seemed a great deal for a smile. But I will say she smiled hard.

In the daytime, we go to the Albion. This is a daytime night club. A juke box plays out of a speaker set that fills the whole wall. It plays *loud!* So absolutely screaming loud you cannot hear anybody speak. You write your order on a pad.

The Albion is a coffeehouse. Tokyo has gone mad for the most elaborate coffeehouses.

The coffee costs 30 American cents per small cup. The waitress gets a percentage on each cup. She wears harem pants and a sort of bra. After you get the coffee (and the music is playing *loud!*), she stands in front of you and dances.

It is the most amazing thing you ever saw. She wiggles. Grinds and bumps. Two feet away. Grind! Bump! Wiggle! The music bangs away with the hottest jazz. Every beat hits you in the back of the head. And at every beat, the waitress bumps at you. Gad!

Overhead, there is a maze of colored lights that turn slowly, making different patterns. The walls are mirrored. In the mirrors there are hundreds and hundreds of reflected waitresses in harem pants. All wiggling.

"Light a cigarette," said my friend. "It is an attraction of the house."

I took out a cigarette. The waitress stopped wiggling. She leaned over and fished a box of matches from her bra. Lit my cigarette. Stood up and began to wiggle.

"This is the morning costume," said my guide. "In the afternoon, the girls wear short skirts with long long black stockings. When you reach for a cigarette, they lift the skirt and fish the matches from their garter."

There is a heavy sale of coffee in the Albion. Packed all day.

You know what? There is an even heavier sale on cigarettes. Everybody seems to smoke a good deal. Wiggle wiggle! Boom, boom! Puff, puff!

Eye on the ball

The other night we went down to Shibuya district in Tokyo to eat the yakitori. Yakitori is so delicious I cannot understand why it has not reached the States. It is a natural for our unnatural barbecue life.

Yakitori is chicken on little wooden spits. It is dipped in a mixture of soyu sauce and spices and broiled over charcoal. Just before serving, they dip it in the sauce again. The hot dog of Japan.

My yakitori restaurant is full of people and is very lucky. The yakitori proprietor has filled it with good luck signs.

One of the luckiest signs is a little porcelain cat. The cat sits on his hind legs and holds up one paw.

"He call customer. Say, 'Hello, hello. Everybody come in, please.'"

That is the way my yakitori waitress explains it. The cat is called manekki nekko—literally "cat calling." Hi, cat.

When I raise one paw, the waitress comes with a quart bottle of Kirin beer. It is one of the easiest words in Japanese. You just say: "Biru."

We cannot pour our own beer. That would be impolite. We must hold up the glass and the waitress pours.

Behind the bar we have a wish for good luck—the Daruma.

The Daruma is a little round man without arms or legs. It is exactly like the little pushover dolls you had when you were a child. The kind you push over and they bounce back up again.

"We call nanakorobi yaoki. Mean fall down seven time, must get up eight time." That is what the Daruma does.

The Daruma is religious. You buy him from Shinto temples.

Once there was a religious man, Darumadaishi. He had no arms or legs. That is why we have the Daruma doll.

When we get the Daruma, his eyes are blank. The Daruma on the shelf at the yakitori restaurant has one painted eye.

"First we give one eye," said the waitress. "Then make very important wish. Must be big, big wish.

"Wait and wait for wish to come true. Maybe two, three year. If you fall down seven time, must get up. Like Daruma.

"When wish come true, then you give Daruma other eye."

"How do you make the eye?"

"With fountain pen. Or brush. Must be black eye."

When the Daruma has two eyes (and wishes are fulfilled), he will go back to the Shinto temple. The name of the wisher is painted on his stomach. The Daruma goes on the shelf and the wisher drops a contribution in the box.

We do not buy yakitori in restaurants only. We buy it on street-corner stands. It is that simple to cook.

It is sprinkled with "seven-taste pepper." I am going to import a little seven-taste pepper. It is the greatest thing for barbecue since Texas invented the border hot sauce.

It is red-and-black and coarse-ground. It has a wonderful flavor.

We pour a little mound of it on the side of the plate and roll our hot spitted chicken in it.

Before we have the spitted chicken chunks, we have spitted ground chicken patties. About the size of a half dollar. Sometimes we have spitted chicken liver, too. We eat a lot. Last night I ate 15 sticks of yakitori.

The manekki nekko cat was very happy with me. He gave me a happy wave-off.

Personal appearance

In the lanterned, antique streets of Kyoto, we looked up Mitsuko Yoshida.

Mitsuko is a butterball Japanese doll. A little less than five feet, 110 pounds. She is famous among Kyoto bathhouse girls as the lady who bathed Marlon Brando. It is hard to top that.

"When Mollon Brando is coming Mimatsu bathhouse, all girls running to tell me, 'Oh, upstairs Mollon Brando!' They very excite."

Mr. Brando was on location. The film *Sayonara* was shot on the canal banks in Kyoto. Mitsuko, among 35 girls in Mimatsu bathhouse, draws Americans because she speaks English. GI English. The result of a *Sayonara* love affair with a Pennsylvania platoon sergeant.

"And what did you think of Marlon Brando, Mitsuko?"

248

"I am very surprised. He have sukoshi belly."

"Little belly is bad?"

"No. Only I surprise. He very young man to have sukoshi belly."

The bathhouse girls work in pairs at Mimatsu. "When I wash Mollon Brando, I take with me Futaba-san. You know what?"

"What?"

"All girls in bathhouse coming in all time," said Mitsuko. "They asking Mollon Brando prease sign picture. Maybe sign handkerchief."

It sounded like quite a ball. A very personal appearance.

"Was Mr. Brando embarrassed?"

"No. Very nice genterman. He sign. You know what he show me?"

"My dear girl! I write for nice family newspaper."

"He show me," said Mitsuko, "his nose. He have funny nose, Mollon Brando. He can push one side, then other side. Then he smash flat. His nose have no bone. Very funny, ne?"

"A boffola. We can print that."

"You know what I think?" said Mitsuko. "I think Mollon Brando like small boy. He all time playing. Laugh and push nose one side, then other side."

You know what I think? I think Mollon Brando have plenty poise. That is what I think of a man who can sign autographs, bare as a radish. And at the same time push his nose from one side to the other.

"Mitsuko," I said. "Let us get on the professional side of this subject. What kind of massage did you give him?"

"First I put in steam bath. He like very hot. Then we give him Japanese bath. Then massage. He like very *hard*

249

massage. 'Can do harder?' he telling me. You know what I do?"

"Hit him with a baseball bat?"

"Nevah hoppen. I do with foot. I get up and walk on Mollon Brando back." (The foot massage is quite a thing in a Japanese bathhouse.)

"And now you are famous? Many girls ask you about this?"

"All girls! Asking about Mollon Brando."

"What do you tell them, Mitsuko?"

"Tell them about Mollon Brando nose," said Mitsuko primly.

Sayonara

In Kyoto, they made a good many scenes of *Sayonara*. Though the company did not get all the co-operation they would have liked. Japan did not care too much for the Michener book or the picture. Not officially. They liked it at the box office, though.

"I see three times," said Mitsuko.

The old Japanese town was spared by American bombers. It has about a million people and three whooping geisha districts. This is the traditional home of the honorable geisha.

Three geisha troupes are playing the local theatres at this time.

It is one of the great towns for Japanese gentlemen on the loose. On the expense account.

One of the most interesting shops in Tokyo is in Tokyo Central Railroad Station. It specializes in gifts from various towns in Japan.

When the Japanese honorable gentleman comes back from Kyoto, he rushes to this shop.

He tells them the name of the town he was supposed to be in.

The shopkeeper reaches on the shelf and takes down a gift that is typical of this town. He gets out wrapping paper of an actual shop in that town. He sets back the date on a little date stamp.

He wraps the package in the special paper. And he dates it back a couple of days. The Japanese honorable gent takes it home to his honorable wife.

"A little present I picked up while visiting the factory town," he says.

The honorable wife is overcome to have such an honorable husband.

We stay at the Doi Hotel in Kyoto. It is so private that you must be introduced to get a room. It is the most elegant hotel I have seen in Japan. But like all Japanese hotels, the beds are so short your feet hang over the end.

It does not matter much since the bed is on the floor anyway.

The problem is keeping your feet and shoulders covered at the same time by the quilt.

A curious thing about Japanese hotels is that you cannot ask the price of a room. It is very bad manners.

You just take the room. When you leave they hand you the bill. Along with a little presento. The bill is always correct. And rooms will run about $10 to $15 including breakfast, dinner and a 10 per cent service charge.

Alongside the door you will see a plant with eight leaves and a thick stalk. It is the first thing planted. It keeps away thieves.

You do not carry any packages into your hotel. The maid comes to meet you at the gate and carries them for you. She sits with you and serves you while you eat.

She takes you down to the gate each time you go out.

You have to be back by 12 midnight. Or turn into a pumpkin. There is no night help. Everybody goes to bed at 12 and they lock the gates. If you want to whoop it up into the small hours, you are supposed to do it in your room.

That is the Japanese custom and nobody minds that at all.

Last night, the Japanese expense-account boys below me went nearly all night. And between laughter and the cat-and-elephant music of the samisen, I was a wreck in the morning. I should have gone down and joined the party.

All the maids at my Japanese hotel came up to help me pack. When I pack, it is a great opportunity to gander my personal effects—they flip for the pocket tape recorder.

This is the day we give each other good-by presents. Sayonara gifts.

The gifts are beautifully wrapped. They have a little colored paper fan pasted on the outside. A gift marking. The maids are doing a little sniffling. It is polite to show a little sadness at parting. Also kind of fun.

My sayonara gift to my maid is a blue-and-white Pan American Airways flight bag. Pan American gave me one with my berth reservation to Hong Kong.

"You no open until we say sayonara." That is what I tell the maid.

It is not polite in Japan to open presents in front of the giver. But she knows by the size what is in the package. In fact, that is what she asked for.

A PAA bag gives her tremendous face. Big prestige.

252

It shows when she walks down the street that she is a traveled woman.

If PAA does not *give* you a bag, you can walk into one of their offices and buy one for a dollar.

Apparently the Japanese do not know this. Because PAA bags are sold on the back streets for $2. Among the American toothpaste and other items black-marketed by American soldiers with access to the PX.

The bag with its overseas travel implications gives so much face that it is even counterfeited.

A great shipment of them went on the market at cut rates recently—they say they were made on the Chinese mainland and smuggled by fishing boats.

The odd thing about these bags is they resembled Pan American bags in color, shape and material. But the side with the wings said *PPAA*. Nobody knows why the maker decided on the extra P. Maybe like a newspaper headline writer: It fit the space more exactly.

We also have a big sayonara at the airport. All our Japanese friends are down to see us off. So are the friends of friends. And the friends and friends of friends of other passengers.

This tends to fill Haneda airport pretty full.

When Japanese say hello or good-by, they bow very low. Many times.

When you get a great many people back to back, all bowing, they bump.

It is very difficult. I feel very foolish when I bow and bump the person in back of me who is also bowing. But nobody else seemed to mind.

In a small bowing country, you must get used to a few bumps. If we were all equipped with chrome and tail fins, the cost would be disastrous.

Planes from Tokyo to Hong Kong take off at night. For you can only make the Hong Kong airport landing during daylight hours.

We took off down the golden strip of runway lights, the big DC-6 climbing over Tokyo Bay with the little ship lights below.

There was champagne and American cigarettes.

And after a while, they shut down the cabin lights and we all climbed into our berths.

And when the sun was up on the blue South China sea, we had ham and eggs and real American coffee. And slid down along the green islands of the harbor with the big slat-sail fishing junks below us.

Over the crowded streets of Kowloon and alongside the Nine Dragon Hills. Onto the steamy, tropical strip at Kai-tak airport.

HONG KONG

The Chinese collar is the equivalent of the American neckline. Chinese gentlemen are not interested in Chinese ladies' legs. When low collars come in, everybody is in a swivet. It is like a plunging neckline.

"Chinese dress cannot open upstairs. Only open downstairs," said the Chinese lady. "Suppose open upstairs, everybody talkee too much."

Gung Hai Fat Choi

The other day was Chinese New Year's. Everybody went around saying "Gung Hai Fat Choi." Which means "Good luck and prosperity."

Everybody has paid his bills and got rid of all the bad luck that got on his tail during the last year. It is the custom to greet the New Year with all new clothing. A fresh haircut, manicure and a bath.

Well, nothing will do but I must have my bath the other day. And so I sent the room boy for soap which arrived in a British tin with red letters.

The soap was jet-black and made a wonderful lather.

Bathtubs are kept half full in Hong Kong. Water is turned off for a number of hours of the day because water is short. When it is turned on again sometimes only hot water comes out. So you keep the bath half full of cold water.

At this time, however, only the cold water was on. I was standing in the cold water and ducking the cold shower. And suddenly it seemed somebody had set me on fire. And I tried to dive under the water and slipped and came close to breaking a leg.

Gung Hai Fat Choi!

256

After a while I got up and dried my tears and looked at the soap tin. It said the soap contained 20 per cent carbolic acid.

The room boy said everybody used the soap.

"Belong number one soap master," he said. He said though that you had to be careful. It was O.K. on the arms and legs. But apt to burn you to a blooming crisp in tender spots.

Due to a pampered childhood, I am tender all over. More so now.

At this time of the year, all Cantonese buy flowers. It is supposed to tell your luck. Good blooms, good luck.

On the last day of the old year, all families must have a meal together. It is important that all members of the family are present.

At midnight, they have the midnight meal of vegetables. For it is terribly unlucky to kill a chicken or animal on the first day of the New Year.

After midnight, children go to the old people and kneel and bow. The elders must then hand them a little red envelope with money in it called "Ngart Sui Chin." Children must not spend the money until after the fifteenth day of the moon.

Most of my New Year information I got from Dr. Herb Wong. He had no work to do.

"It is very bad joss to see a doctor at this time of the year," he said.

All sorts of year-end days were being observed. This day was Officials Day. January 6 was Small Cold Day. January 12 was Meat Pickling Day and a good day to paint your walls.

January 20 was Great Cold Day. Pretty chilly too as I remember.

January 24 was Lu Pan's Day. He is the God of Carpenters. It was a particularly lucky day for marriages.

257

On January 28, the Kitchen God went to heaven to see the Jade Emperor. Tsao Chun keeps a record of what people do in the home during the year. Chinese ladies do not bathe in the kitchen. It might embarrass him.

If I was a Chinese lady I would not bathe anywhere until they changed the soap.

Well, everybody is all bathed and ready to go. Including me with my gimpy leg.

The first three days of the New Year are unlucky. You must be nice to everybody you meet. Even if you know what she has been saying about you at the bridge club.

The third day is Quarrel Day. Most people stay home to avoid beefs. After that you can fall in the bathtub, spend your money, go into debt and run around with flighty ladies again. For the New Year has begun.

All around the town

In the little stands along the waterfront, where the ferries and the wallah-wallah boats run across to Kowloon, they sell hot water by the cup.

In my room at Sunning House, I have a carafe of cold water and a thermos of hot water.

"What for Chinese drink hot water?" I asked the room boy.

"Hot water good for inside," he said. "What for American all time drink ice water?"

This question has put me in a swivet. I may have to go out and get some powdered rhinoceros horn. It cools down the blood. I suppose *you* take aspirin. Now there's a quaint custom!

The lobby of the very stuffy Peninsula Hotel is the afternoon social spot for tea.

It is full of traders and tourists. Airline personnel and Army. Everybody sits around casing his neighbor. (For Hong Kong is supposed to be filled with Red China spies.) Eddie is typical.

Eddie looks like something out of *Foreign Intrigue* on TV. Eddie's business is selling old clothes. He buys old clothing in New York and sells it in the Far East.

"There is a big market for used suits. Good quality but used," said Eddie. "In the Moslem countries some guys don't want to look rich for fear they will be kidnaped. And some places guys don't want to look like they put too much money on their backs. Because the customer thinks it probably is tacked on the bill."

Eddie buys up old clothes in New York. He bales them and ships them out here where they are sorted and pressed for the market.

The Urban Council is having a problem. Since the American Navy has come to the Far East. The Urban Council announces it is in the market for a good street scraper:

"To remove the wads of chewing gum deposited by the world's richest Navy."

The teahouse is the Hong Kong businessman's lunch. The Paris sidewalk café. They open at six in the morning and close at midnight.

During these hours, Chinese gentlemen drop in to drink tea, write letters, do business. They read the papers and check the action.

The teahouses are old and rickety and established like a London club. Chinese gentlemen keep the same table. Year to year, generation to generation.

259

Mention an early-morning stock market break and you get the answer:

"I didn't hear about it. I haven't been to the teahouse yet."

"If you knew Suzie . . ."

Miss No. 48 on the Tennochy Ballroom bill of fare in Hong Kong is a pretty Chinese girl of twenty-three years. She wears the high-collar and slit-skirt cheongsam and has never heard of the best seller, *The World of Suzie Wong*.

The name of Miss 48 is Wai Fun Wong. But she taxi-dances under her English name—Suzie Wong.

I finished *The World of Suzie Wong* on the PanAm plane coming down from Tokyo. I thought it was a real piece of Rover Boys and the hero was a fathead. But the book sells like hot Chinese rice cakes. And the Broadway play is a smash.

You may remember that the fiction Suzie Wong was a Hong Kong night-club girl, too.

The real Suzie Wong has been dancing at Tennochy for a year and a half.

It costs about $1.50 U.S. to dance with Suzie.

She gets a little less than half of this. Her day starts at 6:30 for tea dancing. At 8:30 she takes a break for dinner. She quits at one.

"Then what, Suzie?"

"Cannot sleep. Sometime I play mah-jongg. Sometime read books. About five o'clock sleepy."

"What kind of books?"

"Love story. Boy and girl fall in love."

Suzie Wong said she gets up about one o'clock. "Then sometime go to movies." She adores Pat Boone and is high on William Holden.

260

We went over to Tennochy with Mr. Y. Y. Wong, the playboy of the Eastern world. (Chinese gentlemen love to be known as playboys. It gives a lot of face.)

There are dozens of dance halls in Hong Kong. But Y. Y. said Tennochy was the best. "Prettiest girls. Inwestigate for yourself."

It is hard to inwestigate Tennochy—the lighting is like the inside of a black cat. However, Suzie said 120 girls work there. There was a good band from Manila. Filipino bands blanket the Far East and Filipinos are known as "the troubadors of the Orient."

Suzie dances with Chinese playboys, American sailors, tourists, big spenders from the merchant marine. She can dance anything—bop, tango, samba. You name it.

She has no steady boy friend.

If you want to take Suzie to dinner, you "buy her out." That is, you pay the management the remainder of the evening at the $1.50 per hour rate.

Being bought out and taken to dinner gives a girl face, too. Like marriage, it has a more permanent air about it.

The Tennochy hands you a sort of menu for all this deep-dish apple pie when you come in the door.

Please write (V) in your order, it says. You check off the name of the girls you want. If they are not busy, the head lady sends them over.

There are some wonderful names on the list. Miss No. 1 is Ding Lai Wha. We are also offered Too Cham Har, Ching Ching, Mimi Kwan, Lock Har, Chor Bing Ying and Man Wai.

Miss No. 23 is listed simply as "Mary."

Suzie's main overhead is her wardrobe of evening cheongsams. To Americans, all slit-skirt dresses look alike. But styles change here just like in Paris.

261

"This year collar is higher. So is slit in skirt."

The collar is rounded instead of square this year. It comes right up under the ears. The slit in the skirt is halfway between knee and hip. When Chinese girls sit down this year, they uncover about the same amount of leg you would in a bathing suit.

Chinese men are completely uninterested though in Chinese legs. Collars are what bring them to a slow boil. Americans are the ones who like legs.

"How do you know this, Suzie?"

"More sailors invite for dinner this year," said Suzie Wong, a girl who knows her world.

Slow boat to China

For about 2000 Hong Kong dollars ($345 U.S.) you can buy yourself a sampan and a girl to row it and get in a profitable business. The sampan is the expensive part of the investment —the girl costs only $35.

Last night we went down to the Typhoon Shelter and caught one of these water taxis.

The Water People are a curious part apart of Hong Kong life. The Water People sail the big rib-sailed fishing junks with painted eyes. They run the butterfly-sail lighters on the crowded harbor where the Pearl River comes down from China.

But at night the junks and lighters and sampans tie up in rows as orderly as any suburban street. On the corners of their water streets are the floating restaurants and night clubs, hospitals and churches.

Our sampan had a bamboo and matting roof. One girl rowed a single oar at the front and another used a sculling oar at the stern. Both were Water People—the Dankka who are born, live and die on Hong Kong water.

The Dankka have always lived on the water. A shorter, darker and different breed from the shoreside Cantonese. In older days they were the river pirates.

With translation, the two Dankka girls outlined the business of sampan running.

You buy a sampan. Maybe a fleet of sampans!

You then find a Dankka family with a surplus of daughters. A Dankka girl child costs from $30 to $35. You raise the girl child as a helper on the sampans. And eventually she becomes a water taxi driver.

She lives and cooks on the sampan. If she marries, she raises her children on the sampan. The cost to you is only food and cotton clothing.

Business was booming out on the water. Little sampans went scuttling by with floating delicatessen. The cook sits at the stern with a glaring gasoline lantern hung on the mast.

His stove is a shallow tin trench of charcoal set into the gunwales.

When he gets a customer on the boats, he spins his boat like a lazy Susan—the customer just reaches into whatever pots he likes along the edge of the boat.

Along night-club row, the sampan girls sit out at the front of their flowered sampans, calling out encouragement to the people floating by:

"In here you can forget all your worries and be happy."

At $1 every 10 songs, we hired a sampan with two sing-song girls to float along with us. They played a three-string banjo and a sort of instrument that looks like a zither.

The music is that wailing five-note scale Chinese music. The girls sing in a thin, high voice. And you wouldn't believe what you hear when they play "Seven Lonely Nights."

When the sing-song girls began to jive, a few boats of freeloaders drifted up alongside. Most of them were floating mahjongg players—the oldest floating crap game in *Guys and Dolls* must have been inspired here.

It was quite a sight: the lights reflected on the black water; the thin, high voices and the tinkling instruments; the sampan girls calling. The delicatessen boats drifting by. The big, high-pooped fishing junks with a glow of red light coming through the red curtains.

And after a while, the sampan taxied us back with a steamy, tropical rain beating on the matting cover.

The people you meet

A rainy Sunday in Hong Kong. There are gray clouds hanging over the Peak and planes are droning overhead, awaiting a break in the damp ceiling.

If the clouds do not break, they go up to Formosa. Refuel and try again. Hong Kong landings must be made at daylight or you might push your plane nose into the jagged Nine Dragon Hills that lie on the edge of China.

At Sunning House dining room, the radio rediffusion is playing for breakfast. A quavering soprano singing one of those trilling things you hear in gloomy British resort hotels.

The Chinese having breakfast across the room is a millionaire merchant. He started with vegetables in the market place and parlayed it into chain of hawkers.

He pays for breakfast in cash. The reason: He cannot read

or write. If the waiter knew that he could not sign his name, he would lose face.

She is a Chinese dance-hall girl. Her correspondence list covers nearly every ship in the combined British and American Asiatic fleets.

Exchanging letters is a kind of direct-mail advertising.

"Please send me another picture of yourself," she says in each letter.

She cannot read English. It costs $5 Hong Kong to get a professional letter translator. Sometimes she does not have enough money. If they enclose a picture, at least she knows who it is from.

He is a Chinese broker and millionaire. A couple of years ago, he took us to an expensive dinner. A week later he wired us in Tokyo: "Could you please pay for me temporarily in dollars such-and-such commercial bill and oblige. Your friend."

My friend paid the bill, $500 U.S. It took over two years to get it back. The millionaire stalled and refused to answer letters. He is known as a deadbeat all over Hong Kong. And collectors are told indignantly: "Don't you know I am a millionaire? Get out of here!"

He got into me for a small piece of change, too.

He is a Chinese of great wealth. "If the Communists ever take Hong Kong, my family will be the first to be liquidated." His yacht is ready at all times to go to sea.

Among his possessions is a fleet of great junks running over to Portuguese Macao. The major smugglers' entrance to Red China.

One day we stood on the Macao wharf watching them unload cases. "They will be in Red China tonight," he said.

"What is in the boxes?" I asked. "Bicycle parts," he said giggling. He made a circular motion with his hand as if holding a machine gun. He imitated the sound like a small boy. "Heh-heh-he-heh-heh-heh! Bicycle parts!"

In the hot tenement districts, the refugees weave straw baskets and matting. Rejects from the Nationalist armies. Not wanted on Formosa. A blind ex-captain tends the baby and the mother hauls poleloads of bricks on a construction job.

In Sunning House, the toast is cold and the bacon is too fat. The British colonials eat it stolidy. They dream of home leave where the toast is cold and the bacon too fat.

Marry in haste

The bridegroom never looked lovelier, as we say in the social set. Under the whirling overhead fans of Hong Kong's magistrate court, Madame Chan Kam, fifty-three, asked support from her husband of twenty-six years.

The suit was a big surprise to Mr. Wat-Kam-sang who did not even know he was married.

Today, Magistrate Hinshing Lo handed down a decision.

"Wat-Kam-sang must pay Madame Chan one hundred Hong Kong dollars monthly.

"Wat-Kam-sang was well and truly represented by proxy."

The proxy bridegroom was a rooster.

Nobody got the rooster's name, a terrible piece of journalistic oversight if you ask me.

Mr. Wat-Kam-sang left his native village of Wan Ha in the Po On district when he was seventeen.

For many years he lived under the neons of New York City,

eating at drug store counters far from the steaming rice buns of Po On.

All of this bothered his sister, Yip Wan-tai. Ladies are always trying to get single gentlemen married. And Chinese ladies are no exception to this rule.

Yip Wan-tai looked around the village and decided Chan Kam would make an excellent wife.

The wedding took place with all the traditional ceremony. The court has been digging up a number of people who were invited (and presumably sent the happy couple a silver fish knife or an engraved cigarette box).

Magistrate Lo holds for the plaintiff wife. But out of the mass of witness memory, he had a few remarks:

"There is apparently some discrepancy whether the defendant husband was represented at his wedding by a live rooster or a cake box."

Sister-in-law Yip says it was a cake box, a pair of trousers and a fur hat with a red string.

Other witnesses are positive Madame Chan was married to a rooster.

You would think nobody would forget a detail like that.

Madame Chan, herself, thinks it was a rooster.

Anyway, they agree she was married. And I suppose a lady is in such a swivet on her wedding day, she hardly remembers whether the groom was a rooster or a cake box or even present.

Wat-Kam-sang naturally has been putting up a fair rumble about paying over one C-note monthly. Especially to a lady he has not seen in 26 years. Or ever for that matter.

If somebody is going to go for the C-note, said Wat-Kam-sang, how about the rooster? Let the rooster handle the maintenance.

A husband stands little chance in courts, however.

The bride has taken the stand and testified to her wifely problems.

She has been a faithful wife. She has carried on her husband's ancestor worship. If she did not sew on buttons for Wat-Kam-san, it was because he was not around with his buttons.

"A legal wedding according to the customs of Po On," ruled Magistrate Hinshing Lo.

"Defendant is ordered to pay his wife one hundred Hong Kong dollars monthly. The fact that his sister did not inform him of his marriage is not important."

Mr. Wat-Kam-sang left the courtroom looking somewhat bewildered.

Miss Kindly Perfume

"When I deevawss the General, I give him a new concubine," said Miss Mimi Lau casually.

It was raining in Hong Kong. Mr. Peter Kalischer had come down from Tokyo en route to Burma. Mr. Kalischer is a Far East journalist.

He has a strange obsession. He wants to go to an island named Interview Island. It is in the Bay of Bengal. He wants to see who is there to be interviewed.

Miss Mimi Lau is five feet, ninety pounds and thirty-two years. She is always poking her button nose into an interview. She interviews Nixon and Stevenson and all sorts of admirals.

She married a Chinese general in Canton when she was sixteen.

"Then I find he have the concubine," said Mimi. "He have the concubine and two children."

Even as it happens at the bridge club, Mimi was tipped off

over a mah-jongg game by the commanding general's wife.

"So I take a pistol and go see this woman," said Mimi. "She come downstairs and try to give me tea. But the commanding general's wife push it away.

"If I accept the tea, it mean I accept the concubine," Mimi said.

What she did then absolutely made our blood run cold. She marched the other dolly home. And when the general came home, she said:

"Honey, I want you to meet an old girl friend of mine." The general had to sit there and sweat that one out.

"Afterward I tell him now we can get the deevawss," said Mimi. "But first I buy him the new concubine."

"For a going-away present?" said Mr. Kalischer.

"For a going-away present," said Mimi. "You know what that woman do?"

"Do tell," we said.

"I feel sorry for this girl," said Mimi. "I don't want to hurt her.

"But she talk. She say she make me get the deevawss. I say to myself, 'So you want to play like that! I buy the new concubine. I don't lose face."

"How do you buy a concubine?" we said.

"I interview," said Mimi. "I get the go-between. He talk to mothers with girls. He bring nine, maybe ten girls. I interview. I pay the mother about $500."

On the day before the final divorce papers, the new girl arrived.

"She must come in flower chair," said Mimi. "I have my husband and my mother-in-law. The girl wear black jacket and pink skirt. I wear black jacket and red skirt. That's right for wife.

"She come in and bow to mother-in-law. She bow to me.

269

"She cover her head with red handkerchief. I take little silver concubine stick and tap her on head. I give her new name. I call her Suey Fong.

"I call her Suey Fong," said Mimi. "That's mean Suey for kindly. Fong for smell good, like perfume."

"Miss Kindly Perfume," said Mr. Kalischer.

"I advise her be a good concubine. I advise her be kindly. I advise her be good to the general, treat nice," said Mimi.

"Then I turn to husband. I advise him be kindly to concubine. I advise him treat her nice. I present to him. Then we deevawss."

"An enlightened custom," I said to Mr. Kalischer. "Though I doubt we can tell this in the States. What for?" I said to Mimi.

"I take tea from her," said Mimi. "That mean I accept her for concubine.

"This show all people this other concubine don't make me get deevawss. I get deevawss because I want. I give the general going-away present. I don't lose face."

MANILA

Manila, warm and tropical. With purple-and-gold sunsets filling the sky like the crash of temple gongs. "Where the nila grass grows," it means in Tagalog.

The calesas, the little two-wheeled carts with carriage lamps and ornamental brass harness, go clippety-clop through the streets. The little general store is called a sari-sari store. And the big open-air shops are called bazaars.

The streetside tailor sits on the curb asleep with his head on a sewing machine. And a truckload of convicts rolls through town in a great splash of bright orange jackets and pants.

The warm Manila night

The warm Manila night brings the jasmine smell of the little white sampaguita flower—the Philippines cousin of the tiare Tahiti and the pikake of Hawaii.

On the streets there is a burst of chatter in Tagalog. The moon picks up the men in white, embroidered barong Tagalog. The dress shirt of the islands. A rich smell of Philippine cigars floats in the air. And from the restaurants come the pungent odors of food with exotic names: Pancit loglog; Nlagang karne at Manok; Paksiw na Bangos; Adobong Manok at Baboy.

My favorite town in the islands for its sound—Bongabong.

The dry season is here. In the country towns, the dry farmers parade their saints and pray for rain. In faraway Cotabato six starving farmers died of eating wild cassava.

There is a constant shortage of rice—a controlled shortage that drives up the price. The Chinese control the rice market. Just as they control most business in the Pacific islands.

The Philippines could be a self-supporting country, but is riddled with politicos and big landholders. The legacy of Spanish colonialism, a pattern you find all over the Spanish world.

The violent land: Ilongot head-hunters killed and took the head of a woman tobacco planter yesterday not too far from Manila.

272

Some 8000 guns are loose in the Moro country on the island of Mindanao. A constabulary patrol trying to pick them up is fighting now with 150 fully armed Moros.

It was in the Moro country that the U.S. Army changed from the .38 caliber revolver to the shocking .45 automatic. A Moro, running amok and promised Paradise for killing Christians, could not be stopped by the .38 caliber.

A long-time Chief of Constabulary in the Moro country never carries a pistol.

"A Moro will kill you just to get the gun."

The jeepney is the transportation of the Philippines—a jeep remodeled into a six-seat miniature bus.

The jeepney has a surrey top and is open at the sides. They are painted in gorgeous, intricate designs. Bright blues, orange and reds.

They are very personal property and carry names painted below the windshield: *Victory! Lazy Susie. Balambang Baby.*

I saw a jeepney the other day named "Coca Cola."

The purple-and-gold sunsets lace the Manila sky. We sit in the tropical sea breeze and drink the tangy San Miguel beer.

When American tanks swept down on Manila, they stopped at the brewery. Each soldier filled his helmet with beer.

"Manila was taken on San Miguel," they say here.

I think the Manila rum is better than the rums of the Caribbean. A deep-flavored rum. Flavored with calamansi, the little marble-sized lime of the islands.

Securely yours

"The most unpopular legislation in the Philippines is Social Security," said the Manila newspaperman.

"We do not want Social Security. To grow old in the United States is a horrible thing. But in Asia, man, you never had it so good!"

We were sitting in the cool, tiled corridors of the Manila Hotel. Across the bay, the sky was flaming purple and gold—that wonderful Manila sunset when the heavens explode with color.

"You read in our papers that we have 2,000,000 out of work—25 per cent of the labor force. But what you do not understand is we have built-in social security in our family.

"I am supporting my brother and his family. I have supported them for a year. I do not suggest he look for a job.

"When we were all kids, we lived here with my uncle. At one time or another, twenty-nine of us lived with him. Now he is old, we support him. I have just finished my month and it will not come again for twenty-nine months.

"My cousin is coming up next month from the Visayan islands. He does not worry where to stay. He knows he will stay with me.

"I would do the same with him. That is the Filipino family way of life.

"You know," said the Manila newspaperman, "I used to be a college professor. For nine months of the year, I had a salary. During three months vacation I was not paid a centavo.

"Do you know I used to look forward to the unpaid months? For nine months I lived miserably on my little salary. But, man, when I was off salary I lived with my family! I lived wonderfully!

"When I grow old, I will live with my children. I do not tell them: 'I am good to you now. You must be good to me when I am old.' That is built into them up here." He tapped his forehead.

274

"Do you know there is not a single home for old people in the islands? We have hospitals for TB and for lepers. But not any hospitals for the disease of age. When we are old we live with our families.

"When we are old, our children give us the best room in the house. We are asked our opinions. We get the best food and the first seat at the table.

"The people we support now and their children come by. 'Papa,' they say, 'we won a little money at the cockfight and bet some for you. Here is your share.'

"They did not win at the cockfight. It is an excuse to give you some money. Man, in the Philippines we look forward to old age. It is wonderful."

The Congressman

Congressman J. Nuyda was returning from a trip around the world. He had a wonderful time and got into all sorts of strange difficulties.

He had never been in a Stateside cafeteria before.

"I was sitting there ahnd sitting there ahnd waiting for a waiter. 'By golly,' I thought, 'these must be the bad race relations I have read about.' "

The Philippine consul-general in San Francisco had just gone through a minor scandal.

"By golly," said Congressman Nuyda, "I thought maybe these people are mad at me for that. After a while," said the Congressman, "I saw some people go by weeth their own trays. So I found out."

He laughed a lot and slapped me on the arm. The arm where I had just been shot for cholera.

"There were two of us," said the Congressman. "We made especial treep for the President. To look at our legations.

"We were een Macy's een New York," said Congressman Nuyda. "I was looking at some ties. My friend said: 'Nuyda, here are better ones down thees way.' And he walked eento a full-length mirror. Eet was the reflection of the same ties. Ha, ha, ha."

The Congressman gave me a hearty rap on the cholera puncture.

The Congressman said he was sixty years old. He has 12 children and it was his first long trip outside the Philippines.

He has a taste for good Scotch and a fine sense of humor.

"The Filipina woman ees not like the American woman," he said. "She has no freedom. She ees like the slave. She must not deviate. She must not scrutinize another mahn. We do not recognize deevorce.

"But," said the Congressman, "she controls all the money. You work all day in the rice field. At night you bring her all the money. You may say, 'Please darling, geev me a peso for the beer.'

"But no deevorce. No mental cruelty. She must not deviate.

"Now mahn," said the Congressman philosophically, "ees by nature polygamous. Eef he should deviate, the Filipina woman helps heem. She commeeserates weeth heem.

"But maybe she weel not geev him money. She weel put heem on rations."

The Congressman said he saw his first automatic elevator in New York.

"I stood ahnd stood. I could not find the attendant. Then suddenly the door snapped shut ahnd the elevator started to rise. By golly, I deed not know somebody upstairs pooshed the button.

276

"I told my friend: 'Eef you tell them about thees in the Philippines I will do something to you.'

"We had an audience in Rome weeth the Pope," he said. "Ahnd we had to buy the tail coat. Eet was $75. They took our peecture weeth the Pope.

"When we got to Spain, by golly, all the waiters had the same kind of coat. We looked like the waiter.

"I told my friend: 'Eef you tell on me in the Philippines, I weel cut out your peecture from the Pope. I weel send eet alone to the Philippines.

" 'I weel write them: Look at the Congressman. He has wasted hees substance. Ahnd now he must work as a waiter een Spain.' Ha, Ha, Ha, Ha."

The Congressman banged me once again on the arm and we slid down on the runway between the green cogon grass of Manila.

The maître d'

"My name is Abe, sir," said the maître d'hôtel. "I think I have seen you before."

I said I had been here a couple of years ago. Abe said he remembered it perfectly. He drew out my history skillfully. He swore he read my columns at all opportunities. He is an able man, that Abe.

Out in the harbor, Japanese salvage ships were starting the day's work on the bombed hulks that still lie off the city.

The Japanese are back in business in the Orient. They are bargaining with the Philippines and running cheap shipping on the seas.

The Japanese crews do not come ashore in the Philippines. "If they did, they would be killed, sir," said the waiter. Directly across from my table is the building that was the

Kempei-tai headquarters. The Japanese Army police, the toughest of all the occupation troops.

Directly in back are the ruins of Intramuros. The walled city where the last-ditch Japanese Marines slaughtered thousands of civilians. These things are not forgotten by the Filipinos.

A Filipino official said there was a proverb. (He said he had to think it in Spanish and then translate into English. For Spanish was his first official language.)

"En la vida—In our life there are wounds that never heal, offenses which can never be forgiven. Life is too short to forget them."

"When the Japs came, sir, I ran away," said Abe. "I opened up a little joint on the boulevard.

"They came here. All the big generals, to the Manila Hotel. Yamashita was here, sir. Tojo came here. When the Japanese went away, they left a suicide squad. They wrecked everything. They were here to die."

At the entrance to the dining room there is an inlay of tiles in the floor: VICTORY.

Where the jeepney goes

"We have a saying in Manila, sir," said the driver. "A lady weethout a lubber ees like the jeepney without a driver."

We were driving along Dewey Boulevard. Swinging in and out around the brightly painted little jeeps with the bus back.

"Without what?" I said.

"Weethout a lubber, sir. Weethout a boy friend."

"Without a lover?"

"Yes, sir, weethout a lubber. We have many sayings like that. About the jeepney, sir."

There is good reason, I guess. The annual statistics for the Philippines are released today.

The Philippines hold 21,000,000 people who drive 108,389 motor vehicles.

Seventeen thousand of them are jeepneys. Mostly in Manila.

Where the jeepney goes, there Manila goes.

About the best thing the United States did for the Philippine economy was to abandon the Army's jeeps. They went for surplus.

A whole machine-shop industry sprang up. They put six-passenger bus backs on the jeeps. The jeeps were sold to Filipino drivers.

Today, Manila couldn't move without this volunteer bus system.

Statistically speaking: The 7000 islands of the archipelago were discovered by Magellan.

Magellan was on his way around the world. He stopped to advise the natives he would take over for the King of Spain.

This did not please the natives. Down on Mactan Island, Chief Lapu-Lapu stuck a sharp spear in Magellan. Magellan thereupon retired from the real estate business. Except for six permanent feet which is suitably marked at Cebu City.

There are actually 7100-plus islands. Nobody has ever gotten around to naming 4327 of them.

Men outnumber women in the Philippines. But in six provinces and 150 towns the women outnumber the men.

Residents range from Manila doctors to bow-and-arrow Negritos to Moro bully boys who carry a different kind of sword for every unkind cut known to man.

It is considered great sport among the Moros to sail up the coast and cut up a Christian or two. Today, according to Manila journals, most of the people have moved out of the west coast of Tawi-Tawi.

A few boatloads of cutups are sailing the coast and slicing up the population.

The islands and towns they bothered to name have wonderful-sounding names. Most of them sound like beating on a gong:

Bongbong, Tagaytay, Dipolog, Zamboanga, Dinagat, Panay, Palawan, Balabac and Bulacan. Iloilo, Camarines Sur, Pampanga and Misamis Oriental.

There is a volcano called Hibok-Hibok. And footpads use a short, lethal knife with a pretty name: the balisong.

In the hills near the summer resort of Baguio, the native Igorots eat dog.

In the Moro country of Mindanao, the Moro datus eat durian fruit. It smells terrible but is supposed to make you feel like a permanent twenty-one-year-old. The datus marry quite often. One of them has 250 wives. About 40 jeepney loads.

Fried chicken and bibingka

The other night I had dinner with Colonel Andy Anderson, a wheel of Philippine Air Lines. We ate at the Papagayo.

The Papagayo in Manila is not exactly like Mr. Al Williams' Papagayo Room in San Francisco where I often drop in to check the tortilla action.

I ordered fried chicken. It was my conviction that you cannot go far wrong on chicken or eggs.

Both of these assumptions are wrong in Manila.

"Anything wrong?" asked Colonel Anderson.

I had been chewing for some time. I tried one piece. Then

another. My teeth simply bounced off that bird. It was like trying to bite off a piece of bicycle handlebar.

Colonel Anderson, also an Al Williams aficionado, said I should have ordered Mexican food. He said I was a fool to order chicken and that probably I had engaged the loser at last Sunday's cockfight.

Whoever downed that chicken should have had the Congressional Medal.

Later in the evening I went out and had the bibingka. This is sort of midnight waffle and is so popular I took down the recipe. You can make it yourself if you have a fresh-water buffalo cow in your back yard.

Take a couple of handfuls of ground rice and stir in water until you have a batter like thick cream. Break two eggs in the bowl, three tablespoonfuls of margarine and a couple of spoons of egg and cheese mixture.

The eggs are Pateros or "red" eggs. They are duck eggs buried raw in the earth with a bed of salt. After a couple of weeks they come out solid, salt and red.

The cheese is white and is made from carabao milk. It is delivered in one-pound bricks with banana leaf and bark wrapping.

Now you take an iron skillet about the size of a waffle and pour in this mixture, first lining the pan with banana leaf.

The pan is set on a little clay stove with a very small charcoal fire inside. A flat tin loaded with glowing charcoal is laid on top of the bibingka pan. For a bibingka is cooked from the topside rather than from the bottom.

After a while you sprinkle the top of the cake with a little sugar. Cook it five minutes and serve it with curls of fresh coconut sprinkled on top. The cake rises and comes out rather fluffy.

The night is young

For catch-as-catch-can, booming, sinful night life, I will put Manila up against all comers. That strip in Panama around Kelly's Ritz comes the closest. Paris is for sissies.

It is not elegant. You can get roughed up by bini-boys and have your pocket picked expertly. All within half a block of the best hotels.

You can drink beer in a nipa shack compound. Or gamble in a swank night club, complete with peephole. B-girls hustle in every night club and almost every bar.

Down by the waterfront there is even a soda fountain with B-girls. You like the hostess, you buy her an ice-cream cone.

The elegant district is Dewey Boulevard. The cocktail hour starts on American time.

The sunsets over Manila Bay are the greatest in the world. A warm tropic sky filled with gold and royal purple.

As the sun goes down, the neons come on. And Dewey Boulevard begins to jump. The range goes from Kapit Bahay on one end to Jimmy's with 50 beautiful hostesses at the other.

Both of these are considered fairly class. In between are some of the weirdest deadfalls I have ever seen.

The Filipina B-girl is worth the price of admission. The B-girl spends most of her free time asleep on a table. When she rises to dance with the customer, she gets a blank expression. As though she had been hit over the head with a bamboo club.

She answers in monosyllables. She looks over the floor as though she hopes somebody will cut in. If she sits at a table, she excuses herself within five minutes and goes somewhere else.

As this happened many times of an evening, I began to wonder that I had dishwater hands. But my Manila friends said no.

"They do that all the time."

Out in the Culiculi district, life gets a little richer. Merchant sailors take this in with a sockful of rocks.

The Yellow Bar and the Merchant Marine blast the night with jukebox music. The police walk their beats in pairs.

One of the curious sights of the night is the balut dealer. Balut is a delicacy of the Philippines. It is a duck egg brought almost to hatching and then hard-boiled.

Out in the waterfront park, a block away, the bini-boys not only remove your wallet without your feeling it. They empty it and put it back again the same way.

The bini-boy is something I have seen only in Manila. The bini-boy is a sort of zoot-suit Christine Jorgensen. The bini-boy wears his hair in a stylish coiffure and dresses like a girl.

He braces the passing stranger in a ladylike voice. Zip goes the wallet. If the stranger happens to feel it and protest, he finds he is up against a boy who can hit like a mule.

SOUTH PACIFIC

She wore a coconut hat and a print sarong. Her hair was braided and hung to the waist. Her feet were bare and she could pick up a dime with her toes. Her hips were hung on gimbals—they were that loose.

"The song of the island," I murmured. "An unspoiled child of nature."

"Whatsamatta you Joe? You all time speak the bulloney," she said. "Buy me one Hinano beer."

The happy island

The rains have come to Tahiti—big slashing tropical rains that hammer on the thatched roofs and strike a wild drumbeat on the coco palms.

But it cleared this evening. And we sat near the Auwe lagoon with rum punches. Torches flaring along the jetty and the sound of thunder where the white water breaks far out on the reef. Big smoke-black clouds hung over the neighboring island of Moorea and, below them where the sun was going down, the whole sea was full of red-and-gold fire.

I ran into a couple of magazine photographers at the Hotel Les Tropiques, a couple of miles out of the French colonial town of Papeete.

They said the arrival here of the Matson luxury liner *Mariposa* was the biggest thing to hit Tahiti in years. All Papeete has been getting ready for the big day. And praying that there would be no rain.

It seems the all-night Lido Night Club is equipped with a plumbing system that goes on automatically every 15 minutes.

"It sounds just like rain on a tin roof," said the photographer.

"Every time it sounded off, the band stopped playing and everybody rushed out anxiously to see if it was raining."

"That is an interesting item of life," I said getting out my

lady gave me a meaning look. (I do not know what it
But all us South Seas writers write like that. I want to
with the crowd.)
cked a white flower behind my ear and began walking
m me with her hips. "Like this. Do like I do."

could no more do like she do than I could fly.
llowed her around with my ear full of flowers, feel-
. It is my opinion that you could not even start on
gram unless you were ginned to the eyeballs.
hile, she got me in a corner, where she lifted her
ntly. (Another way we write in the South Pacific.
rite stuff without something about "innocently.")
me how her knees went.
s are bent. Spread them, knock them together.
n the balls of the feet. This ball of the foot gives
lance, so your back part quivers quite easily. The
er of control.
self. Feet together, knees apart. After you get
begin to move your feet with little stamping
shifts you from one hip to the other.
g my bedtime, I said, "Thank you, mam'selle."
e.
t downtown to breakfast in the cool morning,
till going on. The Tahitian lady was teaching
to hula. A fickle kid is my guess.

moa?

get a choice of two tropical guest houses at
of Western Samoa. Aggie Grey's or the
They are not imposing, but the country is
ice is right.

notebook. "Is that the gentlemen's lounge or the ladies'
lounge?"

"It depends," said the photographer vaguely. "It is not like
the States around here and it sort of depends on who is there.
These are kind of mixed-up kids down here and when the
Lido is full you can hardly tell."

They said the hula teams had been working night and day
for the big arrival and were shaking with fright.

They were shaking with something all right.

The Tahitian hula is a hip movement you wouldn't believe.
A local rock-and-roll that reminds me a good deal of my washing machine when it gets off beat and begins to shake the
house.

The big white *Mariposa* followed the pilot boat through
the reef opening and nudged up alongside the dock, where
just about all of Papeete stood outside a roped-off area for the
dancers.

They came out bouncing and jerking—the drums ripping
out a rhythm like a machine gun. The grass skirts were cream-
white. And the pretty brown girls wore crowns of frangipani
flowers.

The 365 passengers were smothered in leis. They then went
ashore and proceeded either to fall in love with the place or
hate it.

The Los Angeles couple was back in half an hour. They
announced they had seen everything, done the town.

"Hot and dirty," they said. "Nothing."

Others went ashore and did not come back for two days.
(Three *Mariposa* seamen missed the ship when it left.)

I went out to the Tropiques and checked into a grass shack.
With some friendly lizards running up and down the wall and
land crabs scuttling for their holes when I passed by.

287

One couple checked in and came out five minutes later. Heading white-faced for the ship. Some sort of crab came out of the house tipping his hat politely just as they went in.

"Slithered out," said the gentleman shuddering. "Big as a dinner plate."

I think the point is none of these things hurt you. You soon get used to them, too. The big spiders eat the mosquitoes. And the lizards eat the spiders. My room is one big happy cafeteria.

And if things bother you, how can you escape the cool sea breeze? The jasmine smell of white tiare tahiti flowers. The boom of the turf. And the drums and the guitars singing among the flaring torches while the little brown girl in the little grass shack shakes cream-colored hips. And even the ladies' and/or gentlemen's lounge rattles like tropical rain on a tin roof.

Lovely hula hips

The night the SS *Mariposa* arrived, they threw a grand fête in the town square under the coco palms in Papeete, Tahiti.

It is a pretty little French colonial town with white water thundering over the reef far outside the harbor. The business houses are balconied for shade. Banana palms grow along the dirt streets where pretty Polynesian girls ride by on put-put bicycles.

The language is French and Tahitian. The Chinese own the town's business as they do throughout the South Pacific. The Tahitians work a little and live it all up on Saturday night. There are fish in the sea. Coconuts, bananas and papaya grow wild. It costs nothing to live. Why work?

It was a bang-up party. Everybo
passengers, French colonial officials,
rock-and-roll Tahitian Hut. Famil
chant ship crews.

We all sat under the warm tro
threw hips in every direction. Th
hips punctuating the punch line

"A handsome fisherman mee
under the earth. Filled with pa
and drags her to his hut, ask

This is the translation of a
program.

For such a lot of hip wig
deal of grace. The grass
poisonous artificial green t
beat out time with tassels

The men sat down in
drums.

The Tahitians went r
floor, they rushed out
in couples.

The tourists went
an agile man to kee
loose hips, I guess y

"Like this," said
Easy."

"Heavenly days
fear such a thing
long would it ta

"Two nights,

"You mean
my bedtime a
in the daytim

The
meant.
keep up
She tu
away fro

Well,
I just f
ing foolish
such a pro
After aw
dress innoc
You can't w
She showed
The knee
Stay a little
you a loose b
rest is a matt
Try it your
this you can
motions. This
It then bein
And went hom
When I wen
the dance was s
some other boy

Want to see Sa

Samoan visitors
Apia, the capital
White Horse Inn.
colorful and the p

The TEAL flying boats stop in at Apia on the way back and forth from Tahiti. It is a fine, comfortable flight over South Pacific green atolls lying in circles of white reef-foam on an endless blue ocean.

It is a short flight from the TEAL base at Suva, and at sundown we landed in a smother of white spray at Satapaula bay. A little boat put out from shore and nudged the side of the big Solent. And we all climbed out and put-putted to the landing.

You drive by car to the guest houses at Apia.

It is a lush tropical island. The Samoan houses are built on mounds. A thatchroof on poles with no sides. You look right through them. When it rains, they let down mats on the windward side.

In front of each house they spike bamboo tubes into the ground and stick flowers in them.

Star dash

Apia, once known as the "Hellhole of the Pacific," lies on a curving strip of beach.

A one-street South Pacific port of flame-red flamboyant trees and curving coconut palms behind a white water reef.

The radio runs a few hours a day, four days a week. There is no newspaper. News reports are pasted on the wall of the post office. There is one occasional theatre and one pool table for the local bloods.

During whaling days, Apia was a roaring sailors' town. But today all Samoans belong to Christian churches—the London Missionary Society is the largest.

The Germans held Western Samoa in 1900. A deal in which

Britain got the Solomons and Fiji. The Americans got American Samoa with Pago-Pago.

After the First World War, the islands were given to New Zealand under a League of Nations mandate. They are held today under a United Nations renewal of the mandate. But independence is due about 1960.

Two strong chiefs claim to be King of Samoa. A point so undecided that both of them sit as chairman in the local legislature.

If independence comes, the islands will revert to a chiefly system that is extremely complicated. About one in every four Samoans is a titled matai.

A High Talking Chief is a chief who talks. Talking being a high-grade accomplishment among the Samoans. Mr. Georgie Jessel would be a High Talking Chief. Also Mr. Gene Fowler when he is in the right frame of mind.

Orating is so important that a visiting speech of welcome is preceded by an orating contest. To see who will make the final speech.

These sessions make our after-dinner speaking look like a brief "hello." But Samoans do not care. One thing they have got to burn is time.

No radio, no newspaper, no TV, no cocktail hour and no cocktails, one pool table. The Hellhole of the Pacific has been somewhat tamed down. About all that is left is for everybody to talk like blazes.

Wind in the coconut palms

A little brown girl named Saruia serves breakfast, lunch and dinner. Afternoon tea, ice, soda. She opens the quart bottles of Tennent's Scotland beer.

Saruia will make somebody a good wife.

"Saturday everybody in Samoa get married," she said conversationally.

"Maybe everybody should stop getting married on Saturday," I said.

These South Pacific islands hold 90,000 people. Samoans are increasing faster than anybody else in the world. And in 25 years, the population will be doubled.

The question is whether a few small islands and a coconut and breadfruit economy can support them.

Nevertheless, I am no man to miss a chance to weep at a wedding. We got a taxi and drove out to the villages. To see how those wedding bells are breaking up that old Samoan gang of mine.

The whole road is lined with trim, tropical Samoan villages. The thatched roof on poles rising from a floor laid on terraced volcanic rock.

There are no secrets in a Samoan village. For you can look right through every house. It is about as private as standing under one of those hotel awnings on upper Fifth avenue.

There were five weddings going on.

The brides wore our regular white veil and dress. But they were barefoot. For shoes kill a Samoan.

The wedding seemed largely a womanly affair. Even as you and I. The ladies of a Samoan village are a ladies' committee of the whole. And, from what I hear, run things in a determined female fashion. The boys sit around in the back room and discuss politics.

The ceremony was held in front of a thatched open house.

All over the front lawn were long rows of banana leaves spread table-fashion for the feast. They were spread under arbors of coconut fronds to keep off the rain. This being the season when rain comes down at ten inches a day.

293

Out in back alongside the rock ovens, there was a stack of enormous roast pigs. They were cooked whole and had an anxious expression. Like a French waiter wondering whether you are going to figure the service compris or are going to be a sport and drop a tip.

The groom had something of the same lost expression. A groom usually has a look of excess baggage about him. And I must report that in Samoa it is the same way.

The village ladies all wore the same color if they came from the same village. Blue or gray or lavender. They looked solemn as ladies do at weddings. And no doubt were dropping remarks like:

"Doesn't she look sweet!"

The taxi driver said Samoan weddings were frightfully expensive.

"Because each family try to do better than the other family."

I gather that if the Smiths fling out ten roast pigs, the Joneses must roast up 20. The ladies' committee is firm on this point. We must pour on the pig even if it kills us.

(If this sounds familiar, I cannot help it. That is the way it is in Samoa.)

Saruia tells me this morning, though, that this is not true.

"Wedding not expensive. Very, very cheap," she said firmly.

I think Saruia will not only make a good wife. She will be a leader in the village women's committee. Her attitude is right.

The rains came

Life at Aggie Grey's Hotel begins at 6:30. At 6:30 a barefoot Samoan girl knocks at the door and brings in the morning

writer with a damp feel. And even the typewriter splashes a little at a key stroke.

This is the Sadie Thompson country. The land of *Rain*.

The back porch of Aggie Grey's Hotel is the dining room, bar, lounge and news exchange of Apia.

Some 30 inches of rain flooded the back yard and I waded knee-deep in floating chickens to my stilted, open-air bungalow. Today the yard is dry.

"Water runs right off," said a banana planter. "Upolu is volcanic rock with a thin layer of humus.

"Why, when they bury a person here, they can't dig a grave. They dynamite it. Which reminds me of a story. You might like it.

"A couple of months ago, they were holding a funeral for a chap and, by Jove, they came to lower the coffin, the grave was too short! Well, there was nothing to do. 'We'll just have to saw old Joe off at the knees,' they said. So they called in the carpenter and made the necessary adjustments."

"Is this a true story?"

The banana planter swore it was right. Right as rain. He said that yes, he would have another. Just enough to wet the bottom of the glass, thank you.

Aggie Grey, herself, presides over the evening splash. A handsome, intelligent woman with a rich laugh.

From long years in a port town, Aggie uses a touch of shipping talk. The help doesn't go to work at Aggie Grey's. They "turn to."

Aggie is the daughter of an English chemist named Swan and a Samoan mother. When she was in her teens, Aggie Swan was famous as the most beautiful girl in the South Pacific.

"I was a young chap then," said the banana planter. "But, by Jove, there has never been such a lovely girl since in the islands."

The back yard at Aggie Grey's is informal. A mass of red hibiscus and coco palms loaded with great, green coconuts. It lies in a bend where the river meets the lagoon and the tropic night rolls with the wash of waves on the sea wall.

Time on a clock dial belongs somewhere else. Day slides into night and night slides into wet dawn when the roosters crow in the thatched village across the lagoon.

"Apia is a quiet town," said the banana planter. "Crime? Well, somebody'll pinch somebody else's chickens, you know. Then they had to pass a law against people sleeping on the highway.

"When it gets down to seventy degrees, the Samoans get cold. And the tarred road holds the heat. Got so you couldn't drive at night. So now you find cases before the magistrate, 'sleeping on the road.' Fine them a few bob. But mainly it's very quiet."

He said yes, thank you. Just enough to wet the bottom of the glass.

And that's the way the time goes by.

AUSTRALIA

Everybody who comes to Australia is daffy over the little teddy-bear koala bears.

The koala bears are very cuddly and kind of dopey.

Well, in the book I read that koala bears live entirely on eucalyptus leaves. This is a hardy diet. But the little koala bear does not mind. In his stomach he has a built-in still. It changes the leaves to a kind of alcohol.

As near as I can figure it out, the cuddly little koala bear is blind drunk. He does not know he is cuddly. Or, if he does, possibly he thinks he is cuddling another koala bear.

Man who came to dinner

As every school moppet knows, Captain Cook wound up with béarnaise sauce on the menu of a Hawaiian dinner.

However, before this happened he got around in a very touristy way. Poking his nose into the Society Islands and around Australia. Asking nosy questions and probably making the natives pose for photographs.

One day in Australia the Captain spotted a kangaroo. The kangaroo gave a couple of hops and pulled a little kangaroo out of its pouch.

"Dig that crazy mule," said the Captain, and, turning to a dusky native, he inquired: "What kind of animal is that?"

The native then replied: "Kangaroo." Which only meant "Good heavens, what an accent these foreigners have." Or something like that.

This is the way the kangaroo was named, according to the books I have been reading. It is a very unlikely story. But then, this is an unlikely country.

Australia is the home of about 50,000 natives called Blackfellows, or aborigines.

The aborigines eat witchety grubs, white ants, caterpillars and clay. Kangaroos, wallabies, wombats, dingo dogs, snakes and lizards. It is a pretty exotic menu.

The most interesting thing, I think, is when they get mad at somebody.

300

When an aborigine gets mad, he goes to the local medicine man.

The medicine man is not like our medicine man. He does not tap the mad gentleman on the chest. Or advise him to eat more fresh fruits and green vegetables. Or advise him not to worry so much and to get a hobby.

No, man, these medicine men are smart.

"You don't like the boss? O.K.," he says, "we will point the bone at him."

He then takes a bone and sings to it. I do not know what he sings, but it is not "Lover, Come Back to Me." It is a mad song.

The medicine man points the bone at the enemy. And the enemy thereupon lies down and dies. Dead as Kelcey's goat.

Our white medicine men shoot the native with miracle drugs. They put him in iron lungs and hold story conferences over him. The native pays no attention. He has been boned and he has had it. He dies in spite of everything. And it drives the white medics wild.

What's for dinner

About a month before I got to Australia, I was having dinner in the London Chop House in Detroit and hearing some gloomy predictions on Australian food.

"The toast," said Mr. Benn Reyes of Chicago, "is as cold as a pawnbroker's eye and as hard as his refusal of your watch. Do not complain," said Mr. Reyes hastily. "That is how I got thrown out of the Hotel Australia."

"Why, son," I said, "surely a punter can take the odds on a steak."

301

Mr. Reyes then got out his pencil and informed me he handicapped Australian steaks about 8 to 5 against.

The other morning I was counting my K-rations when Mr. Jim Bendrodt called me on the blower to have dinner at Sydney's harbor-view Caprice.

Just as I hung up I saw a headline in the newspaper.

SECRET ABORIGINE
TRIBE EATS BABIES

However, your fork-lifting correspondent is no coward. And I arrived at the Caprice at 8 o'clock. Punching the little hat-check boy in the rib fat and inquiring "How much do you weigh, son?"

The boy turned quite pale and muttered something about having to go home to his sick mother.

"And now," said Mr. Bendrodt, "how about some fresh John Dory?"

"I would just as soon not know his name," I said shuddering. "Nor his age or family connections. I am not in the habit of getting acquainted with my fodder. Just bring John along. On a platter."

"John Dory is a fish," said Mr. Bendrodt patiently. "A boneless fish native to Sydney."

"And when do we fry the small fry?" I asked. "After the fish course?"

"Why, that is a defamation on the fair name of Australian food," he said. And then proceeded to bring out blinis with sour cream equal to the Édouard VII in Paris.

I suspect Australian food has changed a good deal.

I had a wonderful carpetbag steak at the Oxford in Melbourne. A carpetbag steak is a sirloin with a little pocket sliced into it. In the pocket they stuff a half a dozen Sydney rock oysters.

At Mario's we ate spatchcock sauté sec with a bottle of the best hock you will find outside the Rhine valley.

At Maxim's I had an invigorating battle with the wine waiter. But the little juicy prawns in half an avocado, with French dressing, was worth it.

I ate Roman spaghetti at Attillio's in Sydney. Filet with a huge cap mushroom at Romano's. John Dory and whole whiting at the Astra Hotel in Bondi. Champagne and sandwiches at Chequers. Chicken livers at André's.

And, I have licked the cold toast problem. Order buttered toast. Australians eat their toast cold and hard. But their buttered toast comes hot. I don't know why. Custom of the country probably.

"Your 'orse 'as won"

The other day I must dust down to Warwick Farm to wager on the cavalry charge. And I came out winners which surprised my Australian friends and me no less.

"What is your system?" they said.

"Hard work and free enterprise," I replied.

Warwick Farm turned out to be a fine grassy field. With many people bustling about peering in little books and gentlemen on boxes under umbrellas crying:

"Seven to two for Blue Meadow!"

Which reminded me I had been advised to give Blue Meadow a cheering hand, betting he would come in either first or second.

I picked a man under an umbrella. And my system for

picking him was that he wore a plaid cap and carried a big white satchel. You may say this is no system. But it occurred to me if my boy should lam out with the proceeds, I could easily follow him by the costume.

"How much do you wish to wager?" he said.

"Why, I hardly know," I said, "being a newcomer. What would you suggest?"

The satchel man looked at the sky. He said the man ahead of me had bet 50.

"In that case," I said, "I will bet 25. Though 25 of what I am not sure. Not being very sure-footed on the local money."

The gentleman then kindly aided me by removing the necessary from my poke and giving me a ticket. At this point I retired to the stands, doing a little private pencil work and finding I had laid out about $55!

"I fear I have just ruined myself," I told the attendant at the stands. "Which one of those animals out there is Blue Meadow?"

"Those are the sheep," he said kindly. "Don't they 'ave 'orses in America?"

"They do," I said. "But mainly to be ridden by the rich. Or by TV people who gallop about on them crying, 'He went thataway!'"

And at this point the loudspeaker cried: "They're racing!"

Before I could really find out where the horses were coming from, they galloped past.

"Allow me to congratulate you," said the attendant. "Your 'orse 'as won."

I then went down and collected from the white satchel man. He was very obliging and said he would take another bet. Though I felt embarrassed to do it to him.

My next pick was a bangtail called Flagtop. And I picked

304

him simply because a gentleman who looked like a bank clerk remarked: "Flagtop? Never!"

Now when I was playing scrabble for the dailies, I interviewed a good many bank clerks in the city pound. Most of them having taken samples to improve their condition and attempting to replace by on-track betting.

If there is one thing I know, it is that bank clerks are the worst horse pickers in the world.

"Give me 25 on Flagtop," I told the satchel man.

Flagtop came home like a gentleman on rollerskates.

I dropped a little on Gold Stakes. This loiterer was given to me by a knowledgeable gentleman. But he failed to inform the horse, too.

"I wish I could stay," I told the attendant. "For I would place a bundle on a very sure thing in the sixth. I must return to the city and write an informative piece about these proceedings."

All of this simply to show you what a cagey horseplayer I am. My sure thing in the sixth was Viteren who is now running— I hear on the radio. He is running and running. The other horses in the race finished some time ago and went out for a beer.

Bottoms up

King's Cross is the Greenwich Village of Sydney, the Left Bank of Australia. Home of the coffeehouses and the delicatessen—a new word in Sydney until the immigrant New Australians brought it here.

It is a lively district of artists and models; pin-up girls and pickup girls. So the other evening I cantered up the hill. To check the action and see how goes the battle against sin these sinful days.

Sydney has been fighting sin since about 1912 when temperance won a round by closing the public bars at 6 P.M.

"Demon rum is on the skids," said the city fathers. For obviously a man getting off work at 5 o'clock could hardly lush it up by 6. Or so they thought.

The Australian is a hardy gentleman. A bearcat in the face of adversity. With only an hour to go, he did his best and he did it well.

The one drinking hour soon became known as "The Five O'Clock Swill." Gentlemen fell out of work and into the nearest pub. Where, if they put their minds to it, they managed to get the blind staggers by 6.

Naturally, this 6 o'clock closing does not apply to the rich. The rich as anybody knows are able to handle booze in the blue-blooded way unknown to the peasants. People with enough scratch simply order their drinks for *all* evening at a night club BEFORE 6 o'clock. Then they go in and stay legally plastered through the evening.

"The same the whole world over"

Mr. George Milne is the manager of the Wentworth Hotel and highest-rating innkeeper in Australia with American correspondents.

"And how do you find Australia?" he asked.

"We have a great deal in common," I said. "We both live at opposite ends of the earth. We both speak English with a hilarious accent. And we both drive on the wrong side of the street. The only place we come apart is on food."

"Australian hotels and Australian food have been badly maligned in America," he said. "They are not truly that bad."

"George, George," I said. "Have you tried your spaghetti sandwiches lately?"

306

I bought a sandwich at the races the other day.

"Spaghetti or bean?" asked the lady.

Ah, I thought, so we are going to rib the visiting Americans?

"I will give with the straight lines," I said. "I'll take spaghetti."

Well, bless your hearts, children, it *was* spaghetti.

"Spaghetti sandwiches," I told Milne, "are enough to make a Navajo turn pale. And I speak as a veteran of the hot-dog atrocity circuit from Ebbets Field to Kezar Stadium.

"Besides it was canned spaghetti. Spaghetti can no more be put into a tin than you are able to can love. It should be cooked fresh to the bite. The Italians say al dente—to the tooth. The bread was as hard as a shoe sole."

Nevertheless, I see Australians banging away at these things as though they might go out of style. And they must hurry.

It is incredibly bad food—cold and friendless.

It takes a real talent to spoil a sandwich. I thought the American Midwest had a monopoly on it with tomato-sauced hamburgers. I am now willing to award the championship to spaghetti between timeless bread slices.

Socially yours

Naturally, columnists get their share of social functions. So the other night I gussied up in dinner squares and dusted over to the Miss Australia contest.

It was enough to make an American press agent weep with envy.

Our Miss America contest cannot compare.

The Miss Australia final was as plush as a charity ball at the Waldorf, and I found myself with several other gentlemen in white tie and tails and strings of little medals on the lapels.

I was about to compare overseas fruit salad with them

307

when somebody led me off, whispering I had muscled in on the Vice Regal party.

I gather this is something like sneaking in the back door of Buckingham Palace and trying to sell magazine subscriptions.

"How do you like our Collins Street?" asked a gentleman.

"I think it is beautiful and tree-lined," I said.

I know this is the answer because I read it in the publicity handout.

Melbourne publicity is run by Ken Macker, the American public relations ace.

In fact, it was Mr. Macker who led me away at this point, explaining that the man I was monopolizing was Premier Henry Bolte.

The Premier, the Victoria Promotion Committee and Mr. Maurice Nathan set up Melbourne tourism. They have set up something called "second-best." I would say it was impossible. "Second-best" in Melbourne simply means that the locals take second best in their own city. Voluntarily. If there are choice tables in the restaurants, the people from Melbourne take the second choice in the rear. Tourists get the choice seats.

It is an amazing show of city co-operation.

Australians are like Texans who are the friendliest, most helpful people I have seen. But I have never seen a whole city back off and let the visitors have the best of everything.

On the half shell

The longest oyster bar in the world is in Flinders Street in Melbourne. This morning I went through two dozen oysters in a matter of one minute, seven seconds. On Sydney rock oysters I will take on all challengers.

308

"The oyster-eating championship of Australia is held by Mr. Joe Barca," said the oysterman slicing open another dozen. "Will you have lemon or vinegar, sir?"

"A little of both if you please. What was his time?"

"The time allowed was one hour, sir. Mr. Joe Barca sat himself down comfortable-like and began. Before the hour was out he had consumed forty dozen. Previous to that, sir, the championship was held by Mr. Harry Nolan, a timber worker by trade. His record was thirty-one dozen."

"That's only a dozen every two minutes. What was the matter . . . lose his appetite?"

"An oysterwoman named May Downie ate twenty-one dozen and four. Will you have some more, sir?"

"Keep opening them," I said. "Is there a prize?"

"For his sterling effort in behalf of the oyster, Mr. Barca was awarded a silver oyster plate and fifty quid. He had a loose throat, Joe did. The oysters seemed to slide down with scarcely a gulp."

I think I could do better than that. I figure my oyster eating at about 50 dozen per hour. I could do better, but I have to take time to put vinegar and pepper on them.

This morning between snacks, I did a little research on the Sydney rock oyster. He is an amazing bivalve. She is even more amazing.

When love blooms among the oysters, the lady oyster goes first class. One million oyster eggs is considered a small family.

The little oysters drift around rather aimlessly until they hook onto something to grow on. The oystermen are helpful. They put out little cement-coated sticks. The oyster grabs hold of a stick and grows. When he grows to bite size they pull up the stick.

The oyster then visits the longest oyster bar in the world.

Possibly wondering what in the world he is doing there. When I arrive, he finds out.

A long time ago

It took me 12 years to get to Romano's in Sydney. It shows what determination will do for you.

I nearly made it once. At that time, I was wearing a correspondent suit and polishing epigrams in a wet and itchy part of New Guinea. The girls were all dressed like a chorus line but were nowhere near as good-looking.

We had a comfortable arrangement with a bomber squadron in Biak. They flew us beer from Sydney. We wrote heroic stories about them.

The proposition to visit Sydney came from an Air Force boy who had drawn the beer run. One story to Kerrville, Texas, papers: one ride to Sydney.

It was on that day they tricked me aboard a wallowing LST. And shortly thereafter we were sleeping in the post office in a Philippine town. The service was terrible. I never quite forgave MacArthur.

"If you ever get to Sydney," said the bomber pilot, "be sure to go to Romano's."

"What is there, cousin?"

"Girls," said the pilot. "And beer. And girls."

So the other night I went to Romano's to shed a tear and drink a beer. And see the girls.

Romano's is one of the attractive night clubs in Sydney. For a city of two million the night-club circuit is rather slim. But night clubs are having trouble all over the world these days.

The décor has been changed, they tell me. Romano's nowadays is mirrored. But the dance floor, once packed with 10-day-leave men, is in the same place.

Later we went over to Chequers, sitting next to Althea Gibson, the American tennis player, and Virginia Paris, who came down to play Bloody Mary in *South Pacific.*

It is a very intimate night spot. The dance floor is about the size of a boxing ring. A five-girl chorus line filled it so completely I thought for a while I was going to be part of the act.

I think I could have done all right. For the talent was meager and the beer powerful.

But instead they called on Miss Gibson who wowed everybody by turning in a professional job of "Hey, There." She had a deep throaty voice and socked it out as though tennis was only her side line.

It has been quite a while since I pressed my pants to fly down to Sydney. Since the days when the ratio of beer to news stories was one bottle, one guaranteed hero.

It took a long time to get here.

"Absolutely everybody goes to Romano's," said the American pilot from Texas.

And I have forgotten his name and the number of his squadron. Or where they went. I wonder if he got back to Kerrville and remembers the big brassy nights in Sydney.

This story would let him know that I finally made it. It may not be like the good old days. But it's good enough for me and I thank him for the advice.

Tea and sympathy

The Australian national pastime, after beer and racing, seems to be tea drinking.

This curious custom should be explained for visiting Americans. So that you don't break the ground rules. Tea is not habit-forming. But once you start it, you can't stop. I can stop it. But the lady who brings the tea won't let me.

This morning, my old carrier the SS *Mariposa* came into Sydney's beautiful harbor. "Filled with American millionaires," said the Australian press. So I must down to the sea. But not without my tea.

"I know you didn't order it," said the tea lady coming into my bedroom and flipping up the shades. "But I thought you might like a bit."

Now I ordered this tea jive several days ago as a matter of experiment.

I ordered breakfast in my room.

"No breakfast until eight o'clock," said the man on the phone. "I can send you morning tea."

"You mean the stuff they bring with the chow mein in the Chinese restaurants?"

"Everybody has morning tea," said the gentleman firmly.

I don't want to be a square. "Send up the tea, Claude," I said.

Now I have few dealings with tea. For my money, the smartest thing the American colonists ever did was to throw a whole shipload overside in Boston harbor. Tea is hardly even served at ladies' bridge parties any more. Most bridge ladies are on martinis these modern sinful days.

The next morning I rose at 6 o'clock. And since there was no breakfast—

"Send up the morning tea," I phoned down.

"You had tea yesterday," said the porter.

"I can only have it on certain days?" I asked humbly.

"You get it every day automatically," he explained.

And this is true, kids. Once you order tea, you get it automatically. In fact, you can't stop it.

I get my tea automatically at 7 o'clock. My tea lady is a cheery soul. She comes in singing with the birds. She is like those hospital nurses who insist on busting you out of your stitches at dawn to rub your back with alcohol.

Morning tea is a pot of tea and two buttered slices of bread.

Once I tried to stop the tea lift. But tinkering with the internals of an Australian hotel upsets everything. I think I got my tea next morning at a gray and yawning 6:30.

Misguided tour

The American tourist flood is about to hit Australia. I gather the Australians shudder a bit to see it coming.

They don't mind the tourist business if only the tourists didn't have to go with it.

"We had a saying during the war," said an Australian, "that the trouble with you Yanks was, you were overpaid, oversexed and over here."

Australians are just like other people, only they drive on the wrong side of the street and walk on the wrong side of the sidewalk.

The American visitor is soon battered so groggy, he thinks it is something he ate.

There are some misconceptions to be cleared up. Australians do not drink tea constantly. Only before breakfast, with breakfast, at midmorning, lunch, afternoon, dinner, after dinner and before going to bed.

Tipping is on the American plan—about 10 per cent. You

313

may tip hotel porters, waiters, chambermaids, taxi drivers, doormen, delivery boys, barbers, elevator starters, waitresses, headwaiters and race-track tipsters.

Contrary to American belief, kangaroos are never tipped.

Speak clearly and slowly. Do not shout at the Australians. They will understand your curious speech, having been indoctrinated by Hollywood movies.

It is an adventure to order morning coffee in a hotel.

If you wish a newspaper, don't bother looking for a newsstand. I run across them now and then but never can find them again. You "book" a paper with the hotel porter. He slips it under the door.

There are 9,000,000 Australians. All of them go to the race tracks on Wednesday and Saturday. There is hardly room for the horses.

When they are not betting on the races, Australians buy lottery tickets. One lottery in Tasmania pays $1,000,000. Winnings are not taxed. I am in the lottery for 25 quid. If I win, I shall settle down here and devote my time and spare money to printing handbills: AMERICAN, GO HOME.

With a million skins, I do not wish to be bothered by tourists snapping my picture and picnicking on my lawn.

Australia has wonderful white beaches and great booming surf. The surf is full of big hungry sharks who will snap off a leg without even calling for room service.

The Australians do not seem to mind. I read in the papers of a gentleman who got his foot snacked off a couple of years ago. Recently a shark whacked off a chunk of leg. "I intend to go on swimming," he said sturdily. Probably not as fast though.

314